BFI FILM CLASSICS

Rob White
SERIES EDITOR

Edward Buscombe, Colin MacCabe and David Meeker
SERIES CONSULTANTS

Cinema is a fragile medium. Many of the great films now exist, if at all, in damaged or incomplete prints. Concerned about the deterioration in the physical state of our film heritage, the National Film and Television Archive, part of the British Film Institute's Collections Department, has compiled a list of 360 key works in the history of the cinema. The long-term goal of the Archive is to build a collection of perfect showprints of these films, which will then be screened regularly at the National Film Theatre in London in a year-round repertory.

BFI Film Classics is a series of books intended to introduce, interpret and honour these 360 films. Critics, scholars, novelists and those distinguished in the arts have been invited to write on a film of their choice, drawn from the Archive's list. The numerous illustrations have been made specially from the Archive's own prints.

With new titles published each year, the BFI Film Classics series is a unique, authoritative and highly readable guide to the masterpieces of world cinema.

The best movie publishing idea of the [past] decade.
Philip French, *The Observer*

A remarkable series which does all kinds of varied and divergent things.
Michael Wood, *Sight and Sound*

Exquisitely dimensioned...magnificently concentrated examples of freeform critical poetry.
Uncut

D0995099

BONNIE AND CLYDE

. . . .

Lester D. Friedman

 Publishing

First published in 2000 by the
BRITISH FILM INSTITUTE
21 Stephen Street, London W1P 2LN

The British Film Institute
promotes greater understanding
and appreciation of, and
access to, film and moving image
culture in the UK.

British Library Cataloguing-in-Publication Data
A catalogue record for this book is available from the British Library

ISBN 0–85170–570–7

Series design by
Andrew Barron & Collis Clements Associates

Typeset in Fournier and Franklin Gothic by
D R Bungay Associates, Burghfield, Berks

Printed in Great Britain by The Bromwell Press, Trowbridge, Wiltshire

CONTENTS

Memory is the Master of Death.
Wole Soyinka, *Death and the King's Horseman*

For Rachel and Marc Friedman,
who carry within them memories
of the past and hopes for the future

INTRODUCTION
. . . .

They put a hundred and eighty-seven bullet holes in Clyde,
Bonnie Parker and the car they were driving. Bonnie was eating
a sandwich. ... I remember thinking at the time, it wouldn't be
a bad way to go, if you have to.

     Jack Foley to Karen Sisco in Elmore Leonard's
     Out of Sight (1996)

Few films in the history of the American cinema inspire more passionate
discussion and generate greater scholarly debate than *Bonnie and Clyde*
(1967). Along with *The Graduate* (1967) and *Easy Rider* (1969), director
Arthur Penn's seductive evocation of Depression era life on the run,
delivered with visual panache and a hip sensibility, ushered in an era
quickly dubbed 'The New American Cinema'. This artistic renaissance,
which energised both the production and consumption of cinema,
resulted from a unique nexus of conditions within the American film
industry and the society which surrounded it: the economic breakdown
of Hollywood's studio system; the shift toward explicit depictions of sex
and violence; the escalation of the war in Vietnam; the aesthetic influence
of European art house films; the creation of a new film rating system.
These three films challenged the moral, ideological and communal values
which had dominated American culture – and consequently its movies –
since the end of World War II.

  From our comfortable historical vantage point in the 1990s, it
seems relatively easy to discern why these three watershed films captured
the spirit of a turbulent America in the late 60s and early 70s. It was an era
lacerated by cultural divisions that grew wider, deeper and more bitter in
the jagged trajectory from the Woodstock Nation to the Weathermen,
from the siege of Chicago to the massacre at My Lai. While none of these
films paints a broad cultural portrait of the social and political issues
gnawing at society's institutions, each encapsulates part of the fierce
clash of cultural beliefs. So, for example, Ben Braddock (the archetypal
college graduate) personifies his generation's fear and loathing of their
parents' plastic existence, judging the existing social order as devoid of
personal loyalty and professional values. *Easy Rider* (1969), which today
seems like a quaint period piece, offers a countercultural alternative to the
stultifying suburbs: a liberating life on the road heightened by the

pleasurable stimulation of sex, drugs and rock and roll. Both films reflect the fears of a profoundly anxious generation that saw its options reduced to early death in Southeast Asia or stagnation back at home.

Yet *Bonnie and Clyde*, the only film in the trio formally set in the past, most poignantly evokes the exuberance, confusion and, ultimately, the deep disillusionment of those times. Screenwriters David Newman and Robert Benton clearly intended their engaging outlaws to resonate with the countercultural sensibilities of the 60s: 'It is about people whose style sets them apart from their time and place so that they seemed odd and aberrant to the general run of society. Most importantly, they did this by choice. ... What we were talking about was what is now know as – The Sixties.'[1] For the new heroes of a youth culture bursting into prominence during this time, acting 'odd and aberrant to the general run of society' was precisely their goal. Their joys and discontents gushed forth in a magical mystery tour of flowing hair, hallucinogenic drugs, war protests, psychedelic music, expansive bell-bottoms, flower power, free love and radical politics. To them, the anarchic Bonnie and Clyde became historical counterparts of their own personal and communal struggles: a young and attractive couple fighting the restrictive moral codes and repressive social institutions of their time.

Bonnie and Clyde fired a shot across the prow of the American ship of state: 'Arthur Penn's *Bonnie and Clyde* was perhaps the first full statement of the new cinema's values; it was as influential on the American films that followed it as *Breathless* was in France or *Open City* in Italy.'[2] By so doing, the film forced an older generation of moviemakers, critics and audiences – all shaped by the Great Depression and World War II – to confront their rebellious progeny – moulded by the assassination of John F. Kennedy and the Vietnam War. It also inaugurated the New American Cinema, a unique period in American film history (1967–80) that, among other stylistic choices, emphasised the visual rather than the narrative aspects of moviemaking.[3] More than its importance to the development of the cinema, however, *Bonnie and Clyde* exemplifies the intimate connections between the creation of great films and the societies which spawn them, even those exceptional films which transcend the eras that surrounded their birth.

Bonnie and Clyde imaginatively mirrored and profoundly influenced American society during a pivotal clash of moral and cultural values. The film itself, along with the public's passionate reaction to it, reflected the intense challenge to fundamental precepts and institutions that shattered the complacent 50s and begot the fragmented 60s: the Hollywood studio system crumbled under the impact of new media; film criticism shifted from stodgy Bosley Crowther to pugnacious Pauline Kael; fashion designers emulated Hollywood not Paris; American visual styles incorporated European aesthetics; film attained intellectual legitimacy; sex replaced romance; conspicuous violence supplanted subtle innuendo; revolutionary fervour overwhelmed moderate political participation; young film-makers wrested creative power from the World War II generation; youthful audiences demanded innovative Hollywood products. Given its distinctive position in the evolutionary contours of American culture and cinema history, *Bonnie and Clyde* must be viewed within the societal framework which generated it and recognised as a vital force in highlighting these acute conflicts and profound transformations.

THE CREATORS

> A photograph is a moral decision taken in an eighth of a second,
> or a fifteenth, or a hundred-and-twenty-fifth.
> Salman Rushdie, 'Ovid Meets hip-hop'

The Screenwriters: David Newman and Robert Benton

David Newman and Robert Benton, the screenwriters of *Bonnie and Clyde*, found themselves working together at *Esquire* magazine in the early 60s, the former as an editor and the latter as an art director. (There, among other things, they created the still-thriving 'Dubious Achievement Awards'.) On the surface, the gregarious, fun-loving Newman, a New York City native, and the taciturn, intense Benton, raised in Waxahachie, Texas, seemed as unlikely a duo as Woodward and Bernstein. Yet they quickly discovered a shared and equally intense love of the movies that dated back to their childhoods. In fact, they spent much of their time thinking about movies, talking about movies and going to movies. Captivated by the zest and spirit of the French New Wave directors, particularly François Truffaut and Jean-Luc Godard, they simultaneously discovered the giants of the American cinema as well: Howard Hawks, Alfred Hitchcock, John Ford and Orson Welles.

But the film that caused them to talk seriously about writing movies was *Breathless* (1960), Godard's first feature. Though utilising a conventional gangster narrative, the French critic turned director dazzled audiences with a liberated visual style that rejected linear continuity and embraced the freedom of unsteady hand-held shots, disorienting jump cuts, stunning long takes, impulsive location shots and vibrant non-star performers.

With images of the love-obsessed, antihero Michel Poiccard (John-Paul Belmondo) of *Breathless* in their minds, it seems natural that when Newman and Benton started banging script ideas off each other, lawbreakers flouting society's conventions became an obvious and engaging subject. Newman and Benton instinctively understood that in the age of Abbie Hoffman, it was cool to be an outlaw. Brought up in East Texas, Benton recollected hearing about the exploits of a legendary duo from his childhood and even remembered how kids dressed up as Bonnie and Clyde on Halloween. Given this background it is not too surprising that, when they actually sat down to write a script, 'the first idea, the very first one, was a movie about two Texas desperadoes named Bonnie Parker and Clyde Barrow'.[4]

As Newman and Benton relate in their 1972 essay about the film's genesis, three factors coalesced to inspire them to move from magazine to movie writing: 1. The overwhelming response to their June 1964 *Esquire*

article, 'The New Sentimentality', which convinced them a new sensibility was omnipresent in American culture; 2. The publication of John Toland's *The Dillinger Days*, whose small section on the Barrow gang prompted them to learn more about the 'professional love affair' that characterised Bonnie and Clyde's relationship; and 3. An Alfred Hitchcock retrospective at the Museum of Modern Art (accompanied by a monograph by Peter Bogdanovich) which gave them an education in cinema at its best.

10   Screenwriter Robert Benton, who grew up in East Texas, was well aware of Bonnie and Clyde's exploits

As a result of these influences, the pair felt the overwhelming need to create films: 'We *had* to make movies the way one *has* to breathe.'[5]

Yet when they actually wrote the various drafts that would eventually evolve into the screenplay for *Bonnie and Clyde*, it was not the radically innovative Godard who influenced them most, but rather his fellow *Cahiers du Cinéma* critic-turned-director, the more emotional and romantic François Truffaut. For Newman and Benton two of Truffaut's films provided lasting inspiration during the entire gestation period: *Shoot the Piano Player* (1960), with its stylish combination of humour and darkness within a milieu of noir gangsterism, and *Jules and Jim* (1961), a love triangle drenched in an atmospheric past which spoke to the problems of the present. All these elements appeared in *Bonnie and Clyde*, though with a decidedly American sense of style and energy quite distinct from its French counterparts.

Eventually Truffaut was offered the opportunity to direct *Bonnie and Clyde* (as was Godard) and, though he ultimately declined in order to make *Fahrenheit 451* (1966), he provided Newman and Benton with a series of crucial visual and dramatic ideas that found their way into the final script. As Matthew Bernstein points out in his illuminating analysis of the script's evolution, Truffaut made many specific suggestions such as emphasising high-angle shots of the swerving car on country roads, playing up the humour of Clyde's humiliating initial attempt at bank robbery, stressing the scenes where Bonnie and Clyde take pictures of themselves, making Captain Hamer a connecting thread in the film, cutting from place to place as Bonnie reads her poem to Clyde, and developing Ivan Moss's hatred of his son's tattoo. Bernstein goes on to note that Truffaut's comments, rather surprisingly, 'focused not on opening the film up to more playful, disparate elements à la *Shoot the Piano Player*, but to unify the film, to give it greater aesthetic coherence'.[6]

Newman and Benton parted company in the late 70s, and both went on to have successful careers. Newman continued primarily as a scriptwriter, sometimes working with his wife, Leslie Newman, and more recently with his son, Nathan. His works include *What's Up, Doc?* (1972), three *Superman* pictures (1978, 1980, 1983) and *Moonwalker* (1988). He recently turned to theatre, writing the book for the award-winning Broadway musical, *The Life*. Benton became a celebrated Oscar-winning director/writer, creating critically acclaimed and popular movies such as *Kramer vs. Kramer* (1979), *Places in the Heart* (1984), *Nobody's Fool* (1994) and *Twilight* (1998). Yet nothing within their long and illustrious careers ever matched the sheer cultural firestorm ignited by *Bonnie and Clyde*. Somehow that first time out of the chute, these two guys 'who knew next to nothing about how such things *should* be done', somehow managed to capture 'lightning in a bottle'.[7]

The Star: Warren Beatty

Following the polite rejections of Truffaut and Godard, Newman and Benton's script for *Bonnie and Clyde* languished. It made the rounds of many Hollywood studios, generated little enthusiasm, garnered no financial backing and, in their words, finally 'went into a drawer'.[8] In retrospect, such a fate seems inevitable; they had written a morally complex and highly nuanced French New Wave film, placing two killers in the main roles and featuring a *ménage à trois* between the three principal characters, for a Hollywood system still tied to the pious Ozzie and Harriet morality of the 50s. The dejected pair felt they had given birth to an unwanted child. Then, some eighteen months after they had originally offered it to Truffaut, the French director was at a party with American film star Warren Beatty. Making idle conversation, Truffaut told the actor about the Newman and Benton script, adding that the title role would be a wonderful part for Beatty.

Beatty had already established his charismatic screen persona as a handsome yet rebellious antihero in such films as *Splendor in the Grass* (1961) and *The Roman Spring of Mrs. Stone* (1961), but from his earliest Hollywood days, he also demonstrated an independent streak that irritated many industry executives. When, for example, no less a figure than John F. Kennedy wanted Warner Bros. to turn Robert J. Donovan's *PT-109* into a film directed by Fred Zinnemann and starring Beatty, the actor told Press Secretary Pierre Salinger that he hated the script and flatly refused to take the role. Beatty also demonstrated his maverick tendencies by starring in Arthur Penn's quirky, experimental film *Mickey One* (1965), an existential allegory more akin to a European art film than to anything resembling a Hollywood commercial feature. As his career progressed, Beatty continued to move beyond simplistic pretty boy parts, eventually gaining critical respect for producing (*Bonnie and Clyde*, *Shampoo* [1975], *Bugsy* [1991]) and directing (*Reds* [1981], *Dick Tracy* [1990] and *Bulworth*

[1998]) films with artistic and thematic aspirations far beyond typical Hollywood productions.

At the time Truffaut told him about the script by Newman and Benton, Beatty was at a crossroads in his career. He saw himself as a tortured iconoclast in the mould of Marlon Brando and James Dean, but the myopic studio chieftains continually cast him in lightweight romantic comedies, proffering roles more suited for Tab Hunter or George Hamilton. After a disastrous pre-production experience with *What's New, Pussycat?* (1965) culminated in his demand to be released from the Woody Allen-written film, Beatty concluded that he needed more control of his own career; he felt compelled to move beyond simply acting in films to producing his own hand-picked projects. Beatty knew no working actors who actually produced their own pictures, but he was adamant about taking his career into his own hands.

So, when he returned to the States, Beatty called Newman and Benton to read the script Truffaut had recommended to him. Within thirty minutes, he told the amazed duo that he wanted to make the film and optioned it. (Beatty initially thought he would just produce the film, envisioning Bob Dylan as the stunted Clyde.) While his role as actor is clearly crucial to the success of *Bonnie and Clyde*, Beatty's function as producer, particularly his interaction with Warner Bros. before and after produc-

tion, is even more important. In fact, it is no exaggeration to state that without his persistent cajoling to get studio approval for the picture, his willingness to risk his professional reputation and personal finances to get the film made, and his post-production insistence on re-releasing the movie after a disastrous initial run, *Bonnie and Clyde* would probably never have escaped its resting place in Newman's and Benton's desk drawers.

Remember that, at this point in their careers, Newman

Warren Beatty between takes on the set

and Benton were struggling neophytes with no Hollywood experience; Arthur Penn's film output (*The Left-Handed Gun* [1958], *The Miracle Worker* [1962], *Mickey One*, *The Chase* [1966]), though critically respectable, still did not contain a certifiable hit. Beatty's clout within the industry derived from his acting not his producing. One story, denied by Beatty but cited as accurate by self-proclaimed eyewitnesses, provides the flavour of his intense ardour for this project. Cornering Jack Warner in his office, Beatty fell to his knees and offered to lick and kiss the mogul's shoes if he would just give him a reasonable budget ($1.6 million) to make *Bonnie and Clyde*.[9] An embarrassed Warner turned him down, but Beatty did eventually strike a deal with Walter MacEwen, the head of production at Warner Bros. Even here, however, his passionate commitment took precedence over business considerations: Beatty agreed to take a meagre $200,000 salary for starring in the film, trading the rest of his standard fee for forty per cent of the film's gross. (Of course, when the film went on to make some $17 million during its 1968 re-release, Beatty's bargain-basement deal turned into a windfall.)

In addition to getting the film financed, Beatty was also instrumental in forcing the studio to re-release it in wider distribution. Jack Warner, who a few weeks after screening the picture sold his shares in the studio to Seven Arts Productions for $32 million, hated the finished product and ordered it buried. Even with an ecstatic response from industry insiders following a public screening at the Directors Guild theatre, as well as a standing ovation at the Montreal Film Festival, Warner Bros./Seven Arts Productions opened it in Denton, Texas on 13 September (traditionally the worst month of the year to showcase new films) 1967, and booked it into only twenty-five other theatres across the United States. According to Richard Lederer, a marketing executive at Warner Bros. who championed the picture, 'it died. It was finished by the end of October. ... I had done my best; I never felt it could be resurrected. I really didn't.'[10] Everyone at the studio agreed.

Everyone except Warren Beatty. Ignoring the vitriolic early reviews of Bosley Crowther in the *New York Times* and Joe Morgenstern in *Newsweek*, Beatty cited Pauline Kael's lengthy and laudatory review in the *New Yorker* (21 October 1967) as evidence of the film's potential to captivate a broad audience of hip, intelligent, college-age viewers. Then, the film became a bonafide hit in London, spawning the first of the clothing fads it ultimately inspired throughout the world. Finally, on 8

December (after the film was no longer showing in the US), a *Time* magazine cover drawn by Robert Rauschenberg brought widespread attention to *Bonnie and Clyde*, heralding it as the start of a New America Cinema; the inside story, authored by Stefan Kanfer, acclaimed it 'The best movie of the year' and cited its importance as equal to American classics such as *The Birth of a Nation* (1915) and *Citizen Kane* (1941).[11]

With this new glut of publicity tucked firmly under his arm, Beatty coaxed, pleaded and ultimately threatened Eliot Hyman, the new CEO of Warner Bros./Seven Arts, to re-release the picture, a then unprecedented event. It was rebooked to open on the day the Academy Award nominations were announced (*Bonnie and Clyde* received ten). Peter Biskind cites a telling example of the dramatic sales increase this time around: at one theatre in Cleveland, the film grossed $2,600 per week in its initial September play date; in the same theatre during its February re-release, it grossed $26,000 per week.[12] With Beatty's indispensable support *Bonnie and Clyde* eventually underwent a dramatic metamorphosis from box-office fiasco into money-making machine, eventually finding itself among the top twenty grossing films of all time.

The Director: Arthur Penn
Arthur Penn represents an intriguing transition between the old and the new Hollywood, though his path to commercial features came via live teleplays and theatre rather than through a film-making apprenticeship. Penn began his diverse career during the so-called 'Golden Age of Television', initially working as a floor manager and associate director on the 'Colgate Comedy Hour' (1951–3). This led him to directing responsibilities for some of the most prestigious television shows of that era: 'Gulf Playhouse: First Person' (1953), 'Philco-Goodyear Playhouse' (1954), 'Producer's Showcase' (1954), and 'Playhouse 90' (1957–8). Because of Penn's extensive experience in live television production, advisers to then Senator John F. Kennedy asked him to serve as a consultant to the telegenic presidential candidate during the famous Kennedy–Nixon presidential debates of 1960. He ultimately directed the third of these historic television events.

During the 50s, Penn eventually aligned himself with Fred Coe, the most important producer of live television dramas during this fertile period.[13] Coe, who also produced Penn's first two features – *The Left*

Handed Gun and *The Miracle Worker* (1962) – encouraged a host of talented young writers and directors to move beyond the limited dramatic and visual constraints of standard television fare. This freedom led to outstanding programmes, many eventually made into films, such as Paddy Chayefsky's *Marty*, Horton Foote's *The Trip to Bountiful* and Gore Vidal's *The Death of Billy the Kid* (the basis for Penn's first feature), as well as other ground-breaking works like *The Bachelor Party*, *The Rainmaker*, *Days of Wine and Roses* and *Visit to a Small Planet*. Coe also brought established stars to television – including José Ferrer, Humphrey Bogart, Lauren Bacall, Henry Fonda and Frank Sinatra – and discovered new stars such as Grace Kelly and Paul Newman. This productive collaboration with the powerful and resourceful Coe provided many dividends for a relative newcomer such as Arthur Penn.

Among his most deeply held artistic values, Coe's devotion to dynamic writing and vibrant acting actively reinforced Penn's veneration of the script's dramatic elements and the performer's subtle craft. As he told me during a series of interviews in Syracuse (New York) and then Stockbridge (Massachusetts): 'A legacy from the theater is you hold the scriptwriter in a certain reverence. ... At my invitation, scriptwriters come to the set. I want them there, and I like them there.'[14] The same respect is evident in his treatment of actors: 'The lesson I learn over and over again is how good the actors are, and what good actors mean to a work. You just learn again and again what fantastic things an actor can do and bring into a situation.' Penn carried these formal values into all his subsequent theatrical and cinematic work.

In addition to his early days in television and his sustained career in the American cinema, Penn has consistently remained attached to the theatre. In fact, he characterises himself as being far more 'instinctual' about theatre productions than he is about cinema. Before he made his first feature, he had already directed the Broadway hit *Two For the Seesaw* (1958). Even during his most productive film periods, however, he continued to direct successful stage productions, including *The Miracle Worker* (1959), *Toys in the Attic* (1960), *All the Way Home* (1960), *Golden Boy…The Musical* (1964), *Wait Until Dark* (1966), *Sly Fox* (1976) and *Golda* (1977). To this day, Penn remains a man of the theatre as well as film: he has created the Actors Studio Free Theatre in New York City, which is devoted to presenting plays out of the commercial mainstream, and currently serves as president of the revered Actors Studio, training ground for many of the most respected performers in the history of American theatre and cinema.

For Penn, the most important result of his theatrical training is a highly developed sense of dramatic structure: 'While a movie doesn't have to resemble a play by any means,' he says, 'to be ignorant of what a play's structure can bring to a film is to be ignorant at your own peril.' And, as Penn himself readily admits, he only left behind theatricality with his direction of *Bonnie and Clyde*: 'In the earlier films, I had been photographing little theatrical scenes. I just knew by the time I made *Bonnie and Clyde* that I was relying on the combination of kinesis, language, attitudes, dance, costume, look, energy, the speed of cutting and internal rhythm as all being elements in the content of the scenes.'

Before looking at how Warren Beatty persuaded him to direct this risky, offbeat project penned by two novices, it is significant to note again that Penn straddles two vastly different film eras: the studio-bred generation of older directors and the young film 'brats' who eventually seized power during the 60s (George Lucas, Steven Spielberg, Martin Scorsese, Brian De Palma and Francis Ford Coppola). Born in 1922, Penn served as an infantryman in Europe during World War II and attended college on the GI Bill, initially at home and then in Italy. He was never particularly enamoured with film as a young man and never studied it formally in school. As he succinctly puts it, 'I don't think I knew a Ford film from a Ford car until I made my first movie.' For Penn, the movie theatre was not a hallowed refuge, not a romantic and isolated hideaway from life and its disappointments, as it was for many young auteurs who rose to prominence during the Vietnam era: 'I didn't go there to indulge my fantasies. It was not sacred for me.'

Thus Penn had far less encyclopaedic knowledge and emotional feeling for the history of the cinema than his younger, more fanatical colleagues. Penn's best films debunk the romanticised individualism of film pioneers such as John Ford and Howard Hawks. It was their style, their economic narrative structures, that resonated in his imagination, and he responded to them formally rather than thematically. So when this East Coast intellectual, this literate man who felt instinctually closer to theatre than to film, found himself directing his first feature (in 1957) on the same backlot as venerable film legends such as William Wellman (*Lafayette Escadrille*), Billy Wilder (*The Spirit of St. Louis*) and Fred Zinnemann (*The Old Man and the Sea*), he was not particularly awestruck.

Everyone associated with the creation of *Bonnie and Clyde* admits that Penn was not initially interested in directing this film, particularly given his recent forays in the byzantine Hollywood studio system. First, Burt Lancaster unceremoniously booted him from production on *The Train* (1964) when his sensibilities clashed with those of the opinionated film star. Next, he endured a totally exhausting and intensely frustrating experience making a big-budget production, *The Chase*, during which his continuous battles with screenwriter Lillian Hellman and producer Sam Spiegel left him physically and emotionally depleted from 'swallowing a daily diet of ignominy'. He was most upset about how Spiegel controlled his post-production work and ultimately recut the film as the producer, rather than the director, saw fit: 'I cannot explain what it is like to have somebody cut the film you shot, the one you had a kind of beat and rhythm to, where they end up emphasizing background and diminishing foreground.' Clearly sick of compromising and with a sizable Broadway hit (*Wait Until Dark*) to his name, Penn withdrew entirely from film production, declining even to consider the various scripts offered to him. So when his friend Warren Beatty approached him to direct a film about two 30s bankrobbers whom he remembered as 'a couple of self-publicizing hoods holding guns, plastered across the front page of the *Daily News*', the distrustful Penn was understandably 'ambivalent', 'gun-shy' and 'skittish'.[15]

But, as he was later to do with the studio heads and distribution honchos at Warner Bros., Warren Beatty refused to take Penn's polite protestations as a final answer. Beatty flew to New York and enlisted the powerful aid of Abe Lastfogel, who represented both the actor and the director as head of the William Morris Agency. The three met at Dinty Moore's restaurant and, as the bemused director now relates the scene: 'I didn't stand a chance. Warren can be the most relentlessly, persuasive person I know and, when he joined forces with Abe, a true elder statesman of the motion picture business, I had capitulated by the time Warren had finished his complicated order for a salad.'[16] Yet what finally won over the hesitant Penn was not Beatty's renowned charm or his culinary talent for combining greens and dressing; it was Lastfogel's reliable assurances that he would secure Beatty and Penn reasonable autonomy over the project and, even more essential, that Penn would retain final-cut privileges – a concession that would give him the artistic clout he lacked in his distressing experiences making *The Train* and *The Chase*.

But once he started intensive pre-production work on the picture, Penn grew increasingly uncomfortable with one aspect of the Newman/Benton script: the explicit *ménage à trois* between Bonnie, Clyde and C.W. Moss (originally a far more physically attractive character called W.D. Jones). Penn worried that this sexual deviance would throw the film's emotional balance off kilter and needlessly distance the audience from the two outlaws. Beatty was equally adamant about removing this segment of the story, claiming that audiences would never accept him in this role and, secondarily, noting that it was not particularly good for his image. As scriptwriter Newman says in his version of this much remarked upon deletion: 'We risked alienating the audience from what we so badly wanted – that it would love and identify with Clyde and Bonnie from the outset, so that by the time they start doing violent things, it is too late for the audience to back away from its identification with the desperadoes.'[17] Eventually, the director, star and writers agreed that Clyde should have some sort of sexual hang-up, that they needed to juxtapose his macho bravado with a deeper sense of insecurity. Together, they came up with the notion of his impotence, a character component which fit nicely with all the gun imagery, the external violence and, dramatically, the sexual connection between Bonnie and Clyde.

Beatty also brought another notable participant into the mix: Robert Towne, who would later emerge as a pre-eminent scriptwriter (*The Last Detail* [1973], *Chinatown* [1974], *Shampoo*) in Hollywood and director (*Personal Best* [1981], *Tequila Sunrise* [1988]) of his own stories. Towne, all the participants agree, added several relatively small but dramatically crucial elements to the script and, as Penn characterises it, he 'brought a crispness to certain scenes'.[18] For example, he sharpened the poignancy of the family reunion scene, which Penn sensed should come after the Eugene and Velma sequence, instead of preceding it as in the

Clyde's impotence is intimately linked with his violence

original script.[19] Towne wrote the section in which Clyde, swaggering with manly boasts before Bonnie's mother, brags that, once they have enough money, they will live just down the road from her. 'You do that and you won't live long,' Mrs Parker responds with clear logic. 'You best keep runnin' Clyde Barrow.' That flat, unemotional utterance written by Towne possesses great dramatic power and, after it, characters and audience alike know that Bonnie and Clyde are doomed.

One final member of the production team also demands mention, though her significant contributions came during the arduous process of post-production: Dede Allen, one of the most creative film editors in American cinema. On *Bonnie and Clyde*, as with subsequent Penn pictures, Allen served as a superb technical professional and, equally important, as a sympathetic sounding board to help the director navigate the emotional depths that inevitably occur during the editing process. 'You kind of alternate,' says Penn. 'You pass this weighty ball back and forth like shot putters playing with a sixteen pound shot.' Allen, currently a studio executive, went on to be nominated for two Academy Awards (*Dog Day Afternoon* [1975] and *Reds* [1981], for which Beatty won an Oscar as Best Director), worked with Penn on several films following *Bonnie and Clyde* (*Alice's Restaurant* [1969], *Little Big Man* [1970], *Night Moves* [1975], *The Missouri Breaks* [1976]), and edited many fine features, including *The Hustler* (1961), *Slaughterhouse Five* (1972), *Serpico* (1973), *The Breakfast Club* (1985) and *The Addams Family* (1991).

Everyone connected with *Bonnie and Clyde* has ample reason to rejoice in their decision to participate in its birthing. The film begat thriving professional careers, most lasting more than thirty years, in a brutal business with a notoriously short memory. All the creative midwives (and many other contributors such as Allen, Towne, Faye Dunaway, Gene Wilder, Gene Hackman, art director Dean Tavoularis and costume designer Theadora Van Runkle) who oversaw its protracted release into the world have sustained lengthy, if at times uneven, careers ignited by the *Bonnie and Clyde* phenomenon. But the revolutionary role that *Bonnie and Clyde* played within the Hollywood system, as well as within American culture at large, reaches far beyond the impact it had upon the individual careers of its creators.

THE CULTURAL PHENOMENON

> Each age builds its monuments to memory and calls them art.
> The seeming solidity of the image, however, is constantly
> undermined by our ability to reinterpret, to change, to alter
> it through our acts of remembering.
>   Sander Gilman, *Picturing Health and Illness*

Bonnie and Clyde remains one of the few films in cinema history whose impact was as profound outside the movie theatre as it was inside. Makings its appearance at a volatile juncture in American history, the film both reflected and contributed to the competing moral, political, economic and artistic visions dividing Americans during the late 60s and well into the 70s. These differences, deeply rooted in America's communal consciousness, represented a fundamental battle for the heart and soul of American society, a passionate struggle to define the very concept of what being an American ought to mean. Writing about these divisions as manifested later in the century, James Hunter observes: 'They are not merely attitudes that can change on a whim but basic commitments and beliefs that provide a source of identity, purpose and togetherness for the people who live by them.'[20]

Seen in this light, *Bonnie and Clyde* became a cultural dividing line: where you stood in relation to the issues raised by the film represented much more than the mere acceptance or rejection of one particular movie; it defined an ideological position along the current spectrum of societal debates. In particular *Bonnie and Clyde* impacted upon aesthetic attitudes; the Hollywood studio system; the liberalisation of moral standards; the depiction of violence; the politics of engagement; the youth culture; and the fashion industry.

The Changes in Critical Attitudes

Today it is hard to imagine the critical hornet's nest stirred up by *Bonnie and Clyde* when it burst upon the scene in 1967. Because the fierce debates which erupted between different critical factions often took place along generational lines, they represented a microcosm of larger social debates. Indeed, one could accurately chart the changing attitudes toward the new American movies – as well as to the shifting mores they depicted – by examining the history of the reviews which greeted its arrival. In the pages of newspapers, periodicals and scholarly journals, a new generation of film writers passionately championed the film, using it as a dramatic example of how to reconstruct American film criticism upon new evaluative models of taste, worth and understanding.

There were no conscientious objectors during the explosive critical combat over *Bonnie and Clyde*. This was a holy war to determine the future direction of American film criticism – and of the movies themselves. One side, led by Bosley Crowther (*New York Times*), included critics such as Richard Schickel (*Life*), Hollis Alpert (*Saturday Review*), Joseph Morgenstern (*Newsweek*) and Richard Gilman (*New Republic*), all of whom mounted scathing, and at times quite personal, attacks on the film and its creators. Essentially, the film's foes found it both immoral in its romanticisation of violence and inaccurate in its depiction of history. So, for example, Page Cook (writing in *Films in Review*) characterises the film as 'incompetently written, acted, directed and produced', accuses its makers of 'promoting that idea that sociopathology is art' and indicts all concerned for 'the evil in the tone of the writing, acting and direction of this film, the calculated effect of which is to incite in the young the delusion that armed robbery and murder are mere happenings'.[21] Charles Samuels' opening sentence (in *The Hudson Review*) describes *Bonnie and Clyde* as a 'bunch of decayed cabbage leaves smeared with catsup'. Then, he gets tough. He claims that the film 'slanders society', that the criminals are 'sick, dumb and ludicrous', and that it 'celebrates what we once condemned'. Finally, Samuels situates the film, along with riots in the country's ghettos and protests against the Vietnam War, as part of the deadly moral sickness which infects contemporary life: 'Each form of behavior embodies a similar lapse of commitment to organized society, and in accepting each one we may find ourselves accepting the other. Each expresses the underlying belief that society represents not law and order but only convention and force.'[22] For Samuels, Cook and their cohorts, *Bonnie and Clyde* symbolised the attack of the barbarians at the gates of American life; they saw it as a savage work of insurgent renegades designed to sap the moral strength of modern society by destroying the values that guided and sustained past generations.

The general who led the charge against *Bonnie and Clyde* was the usually rather genteel Bosley Crowther. As the venerable reviewer of the *New York Times*, and thus the most powerful voice in American film criticism at that time, Crowther was no stranger to journalistic polemics; he had, in fact, taken a leading role against movie censorship earlier in his career, defending controversial movies such as Rossellini's *The Miracle* (1950) and helping to shape the landmark Supreme Court decision that incorporated film under the freedom of speech amendment. Yet, for whatever reasons, Crowther was deeply outraged by *Bonnie and Clyde*, writing three fulminating reviews vividly expressing his personal and professional disgust. After a screening at the 1967 Montreal International Film Festival, he attacks the film on aesthetic grounds, noting how its pacing is 'erratic' and its editing 'helter-skelter'. He also disparages the film for being too 'colorful', calling it a 'charade' that ignores the 'misery and drabness' of the Depression. Citing its 'excess of violence', Crowther denounces it as an assault on our sensibilities, castigates it as an

New York Times reviewer Bosley Crowther called the film's characters 'sleazy and moonic'

example of 'reckless' taste, and bemoans that it represented the United States (in a foreign film festival) during these turbulent times. Finally, he is utterly appalled that the film was so 'wildly received' in Montreal and alarmed by its power to excite festival audiences (and by extension film theatre audiences) to be too 'delirious'.[23]

Crowther's second review (14 August) takes a harsher tone and strikes at the film's historical inaccuracies: 'it is a cheap piece of bald-faced slapstick comedy that treats the hideous depredations of that sleazy, moronic pair as though they were as full of fun and frolic as the jazz-age cut-ups in *Thoroughly Modern Millie*.' Clearly preferring the antiseptic antics of Julie Andrews to the darker deeds of Beatty and Dunaway, Crowther lambasts the film for 'blending farce with brutal killings', denouncing it 'as pointless as it is lacking in taste, since it makes no valid commentary upon the already travestied truth'.[24] Between Crowther's second and third review – during which the film opened in New York (on 13 August), was quickly withdrawn from circulation by Warner Bros., and then reissued by the studio – staunch defenders began to emerge and enter the fray.

Kathleen Carroll (*Daily News*), Archer Winsten (*New York Post*), Penelope Gilliatt (*The New Yorker*), Andrew Sarris (*The Village Voice*), Judith Crist (*Vogue*), Wilfried Sheed (*Esquire*) and Robert Hatch (*The Nation*) started to turn the tide of critical opinion in favour of the movie. Two startling events demonstrate how the film inspired a dramatic critical re-evaluation in the popular press. *Newsweek* reviewer Joseph Morgenstern, after initially assaulting the film (21 August) for its bloody scenes and calling it 'a squalid shoot'-em up for the moron trade', recanted his original position and now characterised its use of violence as 'precisely appropriate' (28 August). Even more unprecedented, *Time* magazine, which viciously trashed *Bonnie and Clyde* for its tastelessness and distortion of the facts in its initial evaluation (25 August), retracted its position (citing it as a 'watershed' film), featured it in a discussion of trends in recent Hollywood films (8 December) and praised its virtues. But as the anti-*Bonnie and Clyde* forces found a formidable general in Bosley Crowther, so the film's pro contingent discovered their most powerful champion in Pauline Kael, until that time a relatively unknown critic.

The turning point of the critical battle over *Bonnie and Clyde* came with Kael's 9,000-word review which, in turn, galvanised her own career as the most influential movie critic of her generation. Kael, of course, had her own agenda, and *Bonnie and Clyde* fit it perfectly: 'Her version of the antiwar movement's hatred of the "system" was a deep mistrust of the studios and a well developed sense of Us versus Them. She wrote about the collision between the directors and the executives with the passion of Marx writing about class conflict.'[25] Kael, along with Andrew Sarris, hated the vision of film (and film criticism) propagated by Bosley Crowther's conservative agenda which valued stolid prestige pictures over spirited engaging movies. But where Sarris attacked Crowther personally – accusing him of 'inciting the lurking forces of censorship and repression', aligning him with 'bigots and racists' and castigating him for lashing 'back at the negro'[26] – Kael offers a more general defence of the film on aesthetic grounds. Though she does reproach reactionary movie critics (no doubt Crowther was primarily in her mind here) for wanting 'the law' to take over their job and for seeing *Bonnie and Clyde* as a 'danger to public morality', Kael maintains that we cannot blame movies for the state of the world, any more than we can blame *Medea* for inciting angry wives to murder.

Kael's masterful review, however, moves beyond the specific defence of one movie; it becomes a proclamation of the essential values and aesthetic sensibilities for a new breed of American film critics. First, she rightly dismisses the cavil of historical inaccuracy, citing everything from *Richard III* to *A Man for All Seasons* (1966) to defend artistic licence for pieces based on historical events. She also contextualises the film's violence culturally, arguing that in the age of Vietnam 'tasteful suggestions of violence would ... be a grotesque form of comedy' and that the film 'put the sting back into death'. She challenges audiences to recognise that the best American films inspire passion as part of their claim to being art: 'To ask why people react so angrily to the best movies and have so little negative reaction to poor ones is to imply that they are so unused to the experience of art in movies that they fight it.' For Kael, *Bonnie and Clyde* succeeds, like all great art, because 'audiences ... are not given a simple secure basis for identification; they are made to feel but are not told *how* to feel. ... The movie keeps them off balance to the end.' The underlying power of Kael's argument is her understanding that *Bonnie and Clyde* has struck a contemporary nerve, that it brings 'to the surface what, in its newest forms and fashions, is always just below the surface'. While eloquently defending *Bonnie and Clyde*, Kael simultaneously brandishes new standards for viewing cinema, elements of taste, style and judgment that directly oppose the traditional positions espoused by Crowther and validated by his contemporaries.[27]

Kael's review proved to be the decisive intervention in the war of words over *Bonnie and Clyde*. David Newman remembers how it 'put us on the map' and Robert Towne says that, without Kael's fiery defence, '*Bonnie and Clyde* would have died the death of a fucking dog.'[28] By the time Crowther issued his third (3 September) piece on the picture, he was reduced to defending himself against an angry backlash of his own readers, and the *Times* soon replaced him with Renata Adler – a far younger critic, one more in tune with the contemporary ideas of Kael. Frank Beaver in his book, *Bosley Crowther: Social Critic of the Film, 1940–1967*, provides a comprehensive account of Crowther's dogged opposition to the film and argues that his intransigence played a major part in his dismissal from the newspaper.[29] Thus, reactions to *Bonnie and Clyde* played a pivotal role in changing the national face of film criticism, proving that American movies could attain the same exalted status as European art films, allowing auteurism a foothold into intellectual discussions, and demonstrating that American writing about film had finally come of age.[30]

The Hollywood Studio System

By the early years of the 60s, Hollywood's studio system was clearly in deep trouble. The evolution of television into America's largest mass-market medium, the dramatic rise in theatre ticket prices (more than 160 per cent from 1956 to 1972), the increased production costs involved in producing movies, the ageing of studio stars, the stranglehold of the crafts unions, the series of lavish flops, and other factors had exacted a heavy price: Hollywood box-office receipts plummeted to their lowest level in history, marking one of the few times that Hollywood seemed in danger of losing its control over world cinema. To retain a sizable share of the entertainment market, moviemakers had to recognise their plight and find ways to make their films appealing to a new generation of filmgoers.

The growing popularity of television was the primary factor in the dramatic alteration of the vast studio system. The lure of constant free entertainment accelerated the downfall of the traditional structure of moviemaking that dominated the industry from the 20s onwards. For one thing, television severely shrank the size (by approximately one half) of the moviegoing audience. It also transformed customary working patterns. By the mid-70s, for example, television (production and distribution) accounted for approximately fifty per cent of the jobs in Hollywood, as ninety per cent of prime time television programming was shot on film.[31] Finally, directors trained in live television – including Arthur Penn, John Frankenheimer, Sidney Lumet and many others – eventually made their way to Hollywood and added a new element of creativity to film-making.

Because television programmes usurped the role of commercial films as the main form of communal entertainment for the American masses, Hollywood producers employed innovative devices to entice viewers out of their comfortable reclining chairs, including technological advances (such as larger screens and better colour) and promotional gimmicks (three-dimensional films). Producers also realised that to lure viewers back to the movie theatres, they had to aim their films at specific audiences and offer more adult entertainment. So they put stories and scenes on the screen that would not be allowed in the cosy living rooms of most television watchers. This struggle for viewers allowed *Bonnie and Clyde*, which would never have obtained studio support in an earlier era, to survive as a unique bridge between the moribund studio-era productions and the emerging independent films.

In his recent essay about *Bonnie and Clyde*, Arthur Penn provides a first-person perspective on how the old Hollywood viewed his distinctive picture. Before the film screening for studio executives, the dictatorial Jack Warner told Penn and Beatty that 'if I have to get up and pee during this, you'll know the movie stinks.' During the first of ten reels, Warner rose, left the room and then came back; he repeated this process numerous times until, as Penn describes it, 'the longest and most diuretic film in human memory finally came to an end.' Even though Beatty tried to convince him that *Bonnie and Clyde* was really a homage to the great gangster films Warner Bros. had made in past decades, Jack Warner's bladder had already passed judgment on the New American Cinema: he decided to bury the film with poor bookings and minimal advertising.[32]

Yet despite Jack Warner's urinary critique, *Bonnie and Clyde* ushered in a revolutionary era of American film-making where auteurs replaced contract directors. Even the most prominent directors of the studio era conceived of themselves as part of a sprawling factory system within which they were well-paid hired hands. Their job was to produce feature films, to fill the seemingly insatiable appetite of American moviegoers. Few had extensive educations or formally studied how to make movies. Instead, they worked their way to directors' chairs by learning their craft on the sets of their predecessors. This generation of film-makers harboured few artistic aspirations, avoided overt stylistic flourishes in their work, and possessed little self-consciousness about their creations. In essence, these men defined themselves basically as storytellers who created popular entertainment for America's masses.

Not so with the new directors who invaded Hollywood during the 60s and 70s. For them, the way they told a story was as important as the story itself. They saw themselves as American counterparts of their European contemporaries: auteurs who brought an artistic sensibility into an industry dominated by a crass mercantile mentality. Their self-conscious obsession with visual style, with how their personal vision was translated onto celluloid, represented a distinct break with the previous era. These film-makers consciously mounted an insurrection designed to destroy the studio system and replace it with more independent production forces; the new film-makers wanted to obliterate the studio system, to democratise film-making so that artistic talent would be a more highly valued commodity than box-office success.

Bonnie and Clyde initiated the first wave of what would eventually become a massive assault on the studio system. It secured the beachhead for the films that followed: '*Bonnie and Clyde* opened the way for a new American cinema that would challenge and energize the classical narratives, genres, and myths of Hollywood.'[33] Think for a moment about just how many Hollywood studio commandments *Bonnie and Clyde* shattered: scripting by two New York magazine writers with no film experience; directing by an East Coast intellectual whose main successes came on Broadway; producing by an uppity actor who sought to control his own destiny; starring an unknown female lead with a supporting cast who looked like regular people; focusing on murderous bank robbers; dealing overtly with female sexuality and male impotence; incorporating technical elements drawn from European cinema; integrating brutality with humour; subverting the values of a traditional genre; ending with the most violent sequence ever committed to celluloid. The fact that it was both critically and commercially successful opened the floodgates to a torrent of provocative ideas, young directors, offbeat performers and innovative movies. As Penn himself recently noted, 'The walls came tumbling down after *Bonnie and Clyde*. All the things that were in concrete began to just fall away.'[34]

The Politics of Engagement
In the late 60s and on into the 70s, the world turned upside down. It was an era of social and political reversal punctuated by an expanding ideological extremism that infused a series of emotionally charged cultural events: the Vietnam War; the Watergate scandal; the assassinations of John Kennedy, Bobby Kennedy and Martin Luther King; the rise of the civil rights activism; the advent of the Women's Liberation Movement. College campuses, traditionally sites of genteel debate and theoretical disputation, became breeding grounds for militant student activism. A generation earlier, these middle-class men and women would have rejoiced in their acceptance to prestigious educational institutions; now, they boycotted classes and occupied administration offices. Political groups such as the radical Students for a Democratic Society (SDS), not elitist sororities and fraternities such as Sigma Chi or Zeta Beta Tau, became the most powerful organisations on campus. Later, as events turned more violent, some bombed buildings and fought pitched battles with campus police. Eventually, they shut down the very schools that had once seemed their surest path to the American Dream. Millions of disaffected citizens came to believe that the rituals and institutions which formed the bedrock of the nation's communal beliefs were sick and rotten. Novelist Norman Mailer spoke for a generation when, in *The Armies of the Night*, he described how monstrous the country and its values had become for many of its citizens: 'She is America, once a beauty of magnificence unparalleled, now a beauty with leprous skin.'[35]

Every segment of the body politic was dissected by questions and confrontations throughout this era. But whatever the personal or political cause under attack, youthful protesters found themselves clashing against the powerful crisscross of institutions that undergird American life: the courts, the military, the educational system and the law enforcement agencies. For the first time in American history since the Revolutionary War, a large group of young, well-educated, white and mostly middle to upper middle-class people found themselves adopting positions which cast them outside the bounds of the traditionally acceptable behaviour sanctioned by their elders. In their eyes, they were highly principled rebels fighting a corrupt and immoral system. Their heroes, however, were not Thomas Jefferson or Abraham Lincoln, but Abbie Hoffman and Huey Newton. In this light, it should come as no surprise that the film characters with whom they most identified were social misfits, spirited outlaws whose dramatic circumstances forced them to fight against a restrictive society. Following the example of *Bonnie and Clyde*, screen criminals of this period were depicted as complicated, misunderstood, often sympathetic victims of society, rather than as the greedy and malignant forces of social deviance seen in previous decades.

Bonnie Parker and Clyde Barrow became the prototypes for these cultural fugitives who characterised the New American Cinema. For audiences filled with alienated students who fervently protested America's deepening involvement in Vietnam, the emotional appeal of this outlaw couple who attacked the status quo on so many levels proved irresistible. And it was not by accident that their activities, set in the Depression era of the 30s, resonated so deeply with the frustrated feelings of the 60s: both eras featured large segments of the population estranged from its government, the earlier era by economic helplessness and the later times by a bankrupt foreign policy. Even though it is situated within an earlier historical period and its conventions place it within the nominal bounds of the crime genre, *Bonnie and Clyde* came to represent a stark depiction of contemporary dissent in opposition to a repressive American system of rules and regulations. The savage execution of the vibrant Bonnie and Clyde at the hands of Captain Hamer's anonymous posse endowed their death with mythic qualities that elevated them into the role of anti-establishment iconoclasts crushed by the ruthless agents of a stifling social order.

The Liberalisation of Sexual Attitudes

Throughout its existence, the film industry has been attacked, on moral grounds, for two overriding issues: sex and violence. Responding to public dismay over a series of highly publicised scandals in the early 20s, Hollywood's most powerful studio heads created a self-regulatory organisation. The Motion Picture Producers and Distributors of America (MPPDA) was founded in 1922 and Will Hays, the Postmaster General of the United States under President Harding, was appointed to oversee it. Most historians view the early years of the Hays office as simply a public relations ploy designed to mollify conservative organisations and to prevent government intrusion into the industry. Although producers were required to submit script summaries to the Hays office for approval, and it did issue a 'Purity Code' with moral guidelines, the office lacked authority to do more than encourage moviemakers to adhere to what was labelled 'compensating values': vice could be paraded throughout the movie, but must ultimately be rejected and defeated by the film's conclusion.

With the explosion of more realistic sound films in the 30s, many of which contained overt sexual activities, America's conservative forces mounted another campaign to suppress Hollywood's licentiousness. Frightened studio executives feared that, unless they monitored themselves, hostile outside forces would invade their industry and compel obedience to harsh censorship requirements. To prevent this, they armed the Hays office with a new and authoritative weapon: the Production Code. Modern scholars now characterise the Hollywood Production Code as an antiquated and hypocritical labyrinth of arcane rules and regulations stipulating what could and could not be shown on American moviescreens. But, unlike the Purity Code, the components of the Production Code were strictly enforced. Hays even established a Production Code Administration, headed by prominent Catholic moralist Joseph I. Breen who sternly oversaw its rigid implementation.

The authors of the Production Code were a Jesuit priest, Father Daniel Lord, and a Catholic publisher, Martin Quigley, and its 'provisions would dictate the content of American motion pictures, without exception, for the next twenty years'.[36] Studio moguls forced film producers to cleave to Code strictures in order to earn the Production Code Certificate of Approval (signed by Breen himself), which was absolutely necessary to secure release and distribution for their products. These stringent regulations required adherence to austere depictions of sexual acts, provocative gestures and specific obscenities. It forbade a wide range of passionate activities and required that the domestic virtues of home and hearth always triumph over licentiousness and seduction. Film-makers chafed against the Production Code and its repressive list of dos and don'ts. But studio chieftains, fearing a moral backlash, insisted on maintaining it, arguing that self-regulation was far better than government imposed censorship.

When, in May 1952, the Supreme Court declared that films were 'a significant medium for communication of ideas' and, therefore, entitled to the same constitutional freedom of speech guaranteed to newspapers, it was only a matter of time before Hollywood pushed the limits of this decision by presenting more overt sexuality on the screen. A scant year later, director/producer Otto Preminger released *The Moon is Blue* without the Code's seal of approval, and its national success demonstrated that American audiences were ready to move beyond the Code's arbitrary regulations. While the film was quite tame by modern standards, merely incorporating some previously outlawed terms such as 'mistress' and 'virgin', it hammered the first of several fatal nails into the coffin of the Production Code.

During the 60s, the influx of 'unapproved' European films which dealt frankly with issues of sexuality, combined with a youth culture that revelled in its sexual freedoms, ultimately forced Hollywood studios to reconsider their restrictive censorship code. Slogans like 'Make Love Not War' and 'Free Love' exemplified the breakdown of traditional moral codes during this time. The arrival of the birth-control pill made the possibility of unwanted pregnancy an almost antiquated notion. Certainly, the college students who made up an increasingly large part of the film audience were swimming in a sea of sexual freedoms that clearly separated them from any previous generation in American history. The result of this attitudinal change was reflected in a new ratings code which debuted in 1968. The Motion Picture Association of America (MPAA) system composed of four categories: G, M (which ultimately became PG and then a middle category of PG-13 in 1984), R and X.

Though the film's sexuality seems quite tame by today's standards, *Bonnie and Clyde* helped push the film industry to alter its censorship policies. It appeared during a crease in time when the old Code was no longer enforceable and the new system not yet in place. The film's initial

Tame by today's standards, the film's sexuality was daring in 1967

scene marks its presentation of sexuality as decidedly different from its American film predecessors. A sensuous shot of Bonnie lying naked on the bed, frustrated by her mundane life as a Texas waitress, openly challenges cinematic conventions of discrete sexuality. A moment later, and still totally nude, she unselfconsciously confronts Clyde from an upstairs window, then she hurriedly slips on a dress and rushes downstairs to join him in the dusty street. Their walk into town culminates with Bonnie licentiously stroking Clyde's strategically placed pistol and ultimately daring him to rob the local grocery store. Penn's vivid imagery and thematic sophistication challenged the authority of Hollywood censors and ultimately forced them to acknowledge a new code of what is acceptable in American cinema.

The Depiction of Violence

Much like the conflicts about sexuality in the cinema discussed in the previous section, violence became an equally important social concern following the coming of sound (1927): a series of gritty urban films elicited an outcry from the more conservative elements in society, including the Roman Catholic Church which established its Legion of Decency at this time. As detailed above, Hollywood responded by establishing the Hays office and, later, arming it with the Production Code, which contained equally strict prohibitions about sex and violence. The Code's strictures were particularly severe about how moviemakers could depict crime. As with rampant sexuality, crime could never be justified and criminals were always punished for their deeds. Though most historians agree that the Code was basically unenforceable after the Supreme Court decision of 1952, it still influenced moviemakers – until *Bonnie and Clyde* simply blew it away in a relentless hail of bullets.

Bonnie and Clyde blatantly shattered every Code decree about portraying crime in the cinema. Even the catch line on the film's poster stressed its combination of romance and violence: 'They're young ... they're in love ... and they kill people.' But what outraged its critics, who viewed it simply as a gratuitously bloody genre piece, was not so much what was presented, but how it was visualised. Many saw Penn's adroit mixture of comedy and carnage as insensitive and, in some cases, downright sadistic; they felt the film treated death with a blasé carelessness, encouraging audiences to adopt an attitude of slick nihilism in place of compassionate sympathy. Critics like Bosley Crowther

Penn forces the audience to feel the film's violence, not just view it

accused him of pandering to the worst elements in American culture and of sensationalising death in order to draw people into the theatre. To them, he was an immoral huckster who glamorised sick psychopaths and turned their much deserved demise into martyrdom.

Penn had just the opposite effect in mind. Making his picture in the midst of the Vietnam War, and following just a few short years after the assassination of President Kennedy, he understood that Americans had become accustomed to watching death nightly on their television sets. Consequently, audiences would no longer accept the antiquated Hollywood conventions of death: violently slain people with few discernible wounds and minimal blood loss peacefully closing their eyes and drifting gently into the sweet hereafter. Far from distancing viewers, Penn desperately wanted them to feel the physical pain and suffer the mental anguish that inevitably accompanies death. His goal for the audience was a deeply visceral, rather than intellectual or even emotional, apprehension of death in *Bonnie and Clyde*.

Bonnie and Clyde became the benchmark for screen carnage: 'the graphic violence so plentiful in modern cinema can be traced back to *Bonnie and Clyde* … and the ultraviolent legacy it bequeathed to modern cinema it helped establish.'[37] In particular, the slaughter of Bonnie and Clyde, their bodies lacerated by a fusillade of bullets, stunned audiences who closely identified with the romantic outlaws. By eliminating the antiseptic conventions of screen violence, the film jolted viewers with brutal images purposely designed to force them to feel the shock of death. Following the final silent frames of *Bonnie and Clyde*, the

American cinema could never retreat to the restrained, discreet presentation of violence that had typified its previous six decades. The film forever altered the polite way directors constructed celluloid death and, as such, permanently changed the relationship between moviemakers and their audiences.

Heated disputes about the amount and effect of violence in the cinema will never disappear – and probably should not. The shocking incidences of children murdering other children in schoolyards across the United States provides a poignant reminder that these discussions reverberate far beyond the realm of academic disputation. But taking their lead from Penn, and ultimately rendering his imagery almost tame by comparison, film-makers such as Sam Peckinpah, Oliver Stone, Brian De Palma, Martin Scorsese, Quentin Tarantino and other less talented directors drench our consciousness with a seemingly endless series of red frames. Even though Penn's use of violence is far more complicated, sophisticated and thoughtful than much of what followed, *Bonnie and Clyde* is still the uneasy progenitor of the cinema of brutality which characterises much contemporary American film.

The Youth Audience

Consider the dramatic demographic shift in filmgoers from the early 50s until the late 60s; the mass audience of the earlier decade had been mostly middle-aged, not particularly well educated, and basically middle to lower class. By the mid-point of the new decade, they were a smaller, younger, better educated, more affluent group. Equally important, their

The film inspired heated debates about the level and effects of media violence

film tastes were profoundly affected by the so called 'Art House' movement: smaller budget foreign films (particularly from France and Italy) that allowed directors a creative freedom alien to the stolid and tightly controlled studio system. As David Cook notes, Hollywood's decline in the early 60s 'resulted from the American industry's obstinate refusal to face a single fact: that the composition of the weekly American film audience was changing as rapidly as the culture itself'.[38] To maintain any significant share of the entertainment market, film-makers needed to find ways to attract these customers.

As the television industry profoundly affected production, so it was an equally crucial element in film demographics and reception. To fight the pervasive impact of television upon moviegoing patterns, producers needed to provide audiences with things not seen on television; before doing so, they had to find out who attended movies regularly and what it was they wanted to see. They quickly discovered that those who had been steady customers during Hollywood's heyday were now staying home to watch television, where the dominant programming recycled genre conventions from the movies – except it was now free. The bulk of the new audience was substantially younger than in past eras. For them, movies still functioned as an essential form of social entertainment that got them out of the house and away from the watchful eyes of their wary parents. And, since they were weaned on television, they brought with them an instinctive grasp of visual communication that far exceeded anything their parents understood about the medium.

The second component of this new film audience was the intellectual filmgoers who related to film as art rather than commerce. Two factors conspired to create this part of the demographic picture: the widespread availability of European films and the burgeoning number of university cinema courses (by the mid-70s, the American Film Institute catalogued over 3,000 film courses at more than 600 universities in the United States). The art films provided the energising jolt of new ideas and techniques, as well as mature treatments of previously taboo subjects; the formal study of cinema endowed students with a vocabulary for viewing movies, an aesthetic and historical context within which they could situate and appreciate contemporary films. These factors conferred a new legitimacy on the emerging notion of film as an artistic endeavour comparable to other sophisticated mediums such as painting, theatre and literature. It was now acceptable, for example, to discuss films by various directors with the same scholarly seriousness used to analyse works by respected novelists. As such, a generation of moviegoers appeared who viewed films as culturally significant, appreciating them as highly developed art forms worthy of academic analysis and intense debates.

Bonnie and Clyde proved crucial in the construction and comprehension of this powerful audience composed mainly of two elements: adolescents and the cultural elite. Its popularity, and the critical controversy it inspired, made commentators aware of the new 'youth market' that would come to dominate American moviegoing. So, for example, when *Life* magazine's Richard Schickel published a collection of his reviews in 1972, he included his initial pan of the film as well as his later reversal. He also pointed out that it was 'the first of the new cult films for kids and helped establish … the youth market', noting that the creation of this market was 'the major commercial discovery of the past five years, the largest single determinant of American film content in the late sixties and early seventies'.[39] Such a realisation threw fear into the hearts of some film-makers and commentators, but it was a fact of life that would forever alter the way that movies were written, directed, produced and discussed.

For the audience coming of age during this time period, as Susan Sontag describes it: 'Going to movies, thinking about movies, talking about movies became a passion among university students and other young people. You fell in love not just with actors but with cinema itself.'[40] Bonnie and Clyde clearly appealed to this youthful audience which saw them not as violent bankrobbers but as romantic revolutionaries. To them, the Barrow gang represented a countercultural alternative, a surrogate family structure that attracted a generation of disaffected youths who rejected the social values of their parents. While not quite a commune, the Barrow gang offered an anti-establishment point of view that proved enticing to college-aged viewers, who were themselves engaged in a fierce battle against governmental forces viewed as repressive and, ultimately, deadly.

The success of *Bonnie and Clyde* demonstrated that it was possible to make serious films that would draw millions of young viewers to the box office and turn huge financial profits. For the film industry, therefore, this market was a potentially vast source of commercial possibilities. Today with symbiotic connections between movies and MTV, as well as

The Barrow gang become a countercultural alternative to stolid middle-class life

the intricate cross-merchandising between film companies and other financial entities (fast food and theme restaurants, soft drink manufacturers, amusement parks, clothing designers, toy companies, T-shirt companies, etc.), the youth market tapped so unconsciously and irrevocably by *Bonnie and Clyde* remains the primary focus of the majority of mainstream films.

The Fashion Fad

Fashion, like film, can be analysed as an intricate and sensitive cultural barometer. Indeed, fashion directly responds to and communicates significant aspects of our personal and communal identity, those aggregate influences that affect our construction of self throughout our individual and societal lives. Put another way, fashion styles both reflect and influence the culture which surrounds them. What people wear during a particular historical period discloses as much about the individual and his/her society as does any feature film, musical composition, painting or other form of artistic creation. The study of fashion, therefore, reveals much about how we interpret and utilise the cultural values which surround us to assemble our social identity.

As such, we might speculate about why the retro 30s dress in *Bonnie and Clyde* struck such a responsive cord in the late 60s, elevating petty criminals from the rural southwest into fashion plates whose styles were imitated by sophisticated men and women across America – and beyond. This was, after all, a time of sexy miniskirts and garishly flowered shirts, of bell-bottomed jeans and flowing earth mother dresses.

Holding up the banks in
style: Clyde

Bras were burned along with draft cards and American flags. The whole
mood of the times seemed geared to liberating the body from the
constraints of clothing, an apt expression of the back-to-nature
movement and the freewheeling sexuality that characterised a youth
culture awash in sensual pleasures of every variety. Why, then, were
women inspired to don berets and lengthen their hemlines to emulate the
style of Faye Dunaway's Bonnie? In what ways did the fashions created
for this movie speak to a generation of women emerging from the fluffy
cocoon of 50s America?

The appeal of Bonnie's style had more to do with the rising tide of
feminist thought in the 60s than with her criminal activities in the 30s. Just
four years before the release of *Bonnie and Clyde*, Betty Friedan's
revolutionary book, *The Feminine Mystique* (1963), had swept the
country and given birth to the Women's Movement. Central to its tenets
was female empowerment and crucial to its aspirations was an
understanding of how patriarchal culture constructed a woman's
identity. Hollywood, of course, proved an easy target for feminist
outrage and contempt. Incensed critics clearly demonstrated how female
screen characters were essentially shallow embodiments of male fears
and fantasies. They angrily derided movies that painted contemporary
portraits of women crippled by their myopic dependence on men and
their superficial domestic concerns. They castigated films that focused on
a woman's bra size and ignored her intelligence. Rejecting these sexist
stereotypes, feminist writers harkened back to the celluloid models of
sexually liberated women in the early 30s, such as Marlene Dietrich and

Jean Harlow, and the working heroines in the later 30s, such as Katharine Hepburn and Jean Arthur.

Bonnie Parker is a complicated mixture of these female figures, a sexually aggressive woman who, finding Clyde unable to satisfy her physical desires, channels her considerable energy into her work: robbing banks. Bonnie's attire corresponds with her evolution from Dallas waitress to career criminal; her garments and style represent a conscious attempt to emulate the Hollywood queens of her time. Early in the film, Bonnie's wardrobe stresses her sexual allure, much as did those of Jean Harlow and Mae West. In the middle of the film, however, her outfits change to mirror the professional and working-class ensembles of the later 30s, imitating those worn by Katharine Hepburn and Rosalind Russell. So, while Theadora Van Runkle's costumes mimic the styles of the 30s, they concurrently invoke the spirit of these strong heroines of an earlier era.

A good example of this spirit can be seen in Bonnie's most influential outfit: the beret set at a rakish angle, the separate blouse and skirt (with a mid-calf hemline) combination – sometimes with a dark jacket set off with a white blouse and other times incorporating a colourful kerchief. Through these clothing combinations, she projects an assertive image of purpose and power, though without forsaking traditional women's attire (as does Dietrich who ultimately dons men's trousers and evening wear). This professional working woman's apparel in the mould of Hepburn and Russell could easily be worn by women in busy offices and swanky boardrooms anywhere in America. These forceful clothes express the power of women while still projecting a

Bonnie's outfits stress assertiveness and power without forsaking femininity

distinctive aura of femininity, thus not threatening men on any conscious or subconscious level.

On moviescreens and in the world surrounding them, women lost large portions of their cultural and economic strength when the men returned home from World War II. American society, at times subtly and at other times far more bluntly, encouraged them to give up the jobs they held during the war, to create homes for their battle-weary husbands, and to raise a generation of post-war children. With the onslaught of political agitation for civil liberties and women's rights during the 60s, following an era which emphasised female docility, new images appeared that reflected the growing dissatisfaction of women with their enforced domestication. Clearly, Theadora Van Runkle's fashions appealed to this new generation of women ready and willing to enter the job force. Yet, given the prevailing dress requirements they faced, most of these working women could not wear the more outrageous and provocative clothing styles of the 60s to their places of employment; they could, however, easily slip into the 'Bonnie Parker look'. By adopting this style, they looked chic and powerful, professional and sophisticated, without appropriating rigid masculine styles that camouflaged their femininity. The costumes in *Bonnie and Clyde*, particularly those worn by Faye Dunaway, had a sweeping impact on the American fashion scene. They presented a distinctive look which, while harkening back to an earlier age of screen heroines, simultaneously rejected the notions of 50s female passivity and allowed contemporary women to display their growing power and emerging confidence.[41]

FILM ANALYSIS

. . . .

Now the Queen of Carthage/ will accept suffering as she accepted favor:/ to be noticed by the Fates/ is some distinction after all./ Or should one say, to have honored hunger,/ since the Fates go by that name also.

Louise Gluck, 'The Queen of Carthage'

Credit Sequence
Bonnie and Clyde opens with thirty-two sepia tinted photographs interspersed with black and white credits. Accompanying the visuals

throughout the credit sequence is the clicking of a camera shutter and, from the point when the picture's title (after the sixteenth photograph) appears onward, the sound of Rudy Vallee singing the romantic love song, 'Deep Night' growing gradually louder. The first fourteen photographs contain an assortment of period portraits of Depression era farm families, much in the style of Walker Evans. We see various shots of parents (and a few grandparents) and their children in different group poses, of ramshackle farmhouses and desiccated fields, and of kids wearing bib overalls and playing on farm vehicles. As the white credits naming the performers and the title appear on the otherwise dark screen, they slowly dissolve to red and then fade into the black background, a grim foreshadowing of the blood and death to come.

Approximately halfway through this series of photographs, the still images shift from family portraits to shots of the historical Bonnie, Clyde and their gang members. At first, these figures seem as innocuous as the farm families, including a jocular picture of three men eating watermelon and another of a young woman posed pensively on a hillside. A violent element soon emerges, however, and then comes to dominate this progression of scenes: in photograph twenty-one, a trio of men stand in front of a shack with their weapons; in twenty-eight, two men lean on the hood of a car cradling rifles; in number thirty, three kneeling men fire their guns down the road at an unidentified object. Finally, the last two photographs juxtapose text with images. Vertical pictures of Faye Dunaway and Warren Beatty on screen right are accompanied by short biographies of Bonnie Parker and Clyde Barrow on screen left.

This short credit sequence beautifully contextualises both the film's characters and its plot. By starting with actual period photographs, Penn firmly situates the film within a particular historical era and simultaneously establishes a beguiling sense of accuracy and credibility for his fictional characters and their actions. In addition, the sequence subtly introduces thematic and visual motifs that Penn interweaves throughout the rest of the movie, including the creation of families, the escalation of violence, the connection between parents and their children, the desperation of the times and the poverty of rural life. Even more importantly, he introduces the concept of visually documenting these moments, of freezing a moment in time and, thereby, preserving it forever. And, of course, he initiates the act of taking staged pictures which plays a significant role throughout the movie.

'The Things That Turn Up In the Street These Days': The Meeting of Bonnie and Clyde

Following the credit sequence, the film begins with an unusual visual moment: an extreme close-up of an unknown woman's lips as she applies lipstick and then licks them to add tantalising moisture. This disorienting image plunges the audience directly into the action, without the comfort of a traditional establishing shot, thus denying the viewer any knowledge of physical place or character identification. (It may also be a sly visual allusion to the famous shot of Orson Welles' lips in *Citizen Kane*; that Bonnie's mouth is shaped into what is generally called 'rosebud lips' adds to this possibility.) When the woman rises, we see she is naked, save for a pair of skimpy panties. Penn's next series of shots clearly expresses this woman's frustration without a single word. She flops down on the bed, hits the bars and then pounds on them; her face rises until it rests, imprisoned, between the bars and ends with a close-up of her entrapped eyes that provides ample evidence of her crippled mental state.

From here, Penn cuts outside the tacky bedroom and his high-angle shot shows a dapper young man casing a car outside the woman's home. When she calls out 'Hey Boy', he turns to find a naked woman, totally unashamed of her nudity, filling the frame of an upstairs window. Telling him to wait, she hurriedly slips on a flimsy dress and bolts down the rickety stairs. Penn situates his camera at the bottom of the staircase, so that when she dashes out of the house, we watch from a low angle, as if peering up her dress. Arriving breathlessly outside and still buttoning up her dress, the woman is somewhat surprised to find him still waiting for her.

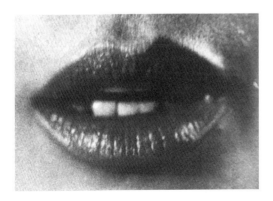

The film's disorienting opening image

At the invitation of the young man, the couple stroll into town to buy a Coke, and the camera tracks along with them. The man reveals he was in state prison and even chopped off two toes to avoid a work detail. Ironically, he was paroled the next day, so his sacrifice represents the first darkly comic moment in the picture. Even though this is Main Street, it is almost totally deserted, filled with abandoned buildings, empty stores and boarded-up businesses – including a closed movie theatre. Again, Penn shows the woman trapped within the frame. As she circles the soda bottle invitingly with her lips, she is pinioned between the man swigging his Coke – an unlighted match bouncing up and down on one side of his mouth – and the gasoline pump of a vacant gas station. 'What's it like?' she asks of the armed robbery that got him a stretch in prison. 'It ain't like anything,' he replies.

This short verbal banter, like so much of the seemingly casual dialogue in this first sequence, provides valuable clues to each figure's character that will be developed and elaborated as the film progresses. The intellectually curious woman wants specific information about how things feel, particularly those actions which promise excitement and the possibility to break out of her boring life. She appears emotionally inquisitive and intellectually capable of delving beneath appearances to deeper concerns. The man, however, lacks her capacity for thinking beyond the surface of events; he answers her open-ended question with the most mundane, amorphous and, ultimately, useless information about these sensations. Throughout the film, this pattern emerges over and over again. The innately perceptive Bonnie struggles to express the significant implications and emotional toll their activities exact on their relationship, while the basically inarticulate Clyde rarely raises his consciousness beyond planning the physical details of their life together. In fact, in the first crime committed after they meet, it is Bonnie who challenges Clyde with not having the 'gumption' to use the gun, daring him to rob Ritters corner grocery store.

Following the grocery store hold-up, they steal a car and, accompanied by Flatt and Scrugg's bluegrass rendition of 'Foggy Mountain Breakdown', make their getaway, after finally introducing themselves to each other and the audience. Careening from side to side down a dusty road in their stolen vehicle, an obviously stimulated Bonnie excitedly hugs and kisses Clyde as he steers around oncoming vehicles and struggles to keep the car on the road. Finally, he parks in a deserted patch of green, first cajoling her 'to slow down' and 'take it easy', then thrusting her aside and demanding that she 'cut it out', and finally bolting from the car and limping away into the field. 'I ain't much of a lover boy,' he tells her. 'I never saw the percentage in it.' 'Ain't nothing wrong with me' he quickly adds with a goofy grin, followed by 'I don't like boys or anything' as he tries to extract his head through the window and comically bangs it on the car roof. The flustered Bonnie, lighting her cigarette, can only muster the observation that 'Your advertising is just dandy. Folks just never guess you didn't have a thing to sell.'

This sequence releases the suppressed sexuality which has oozed, barely contained, just beneath the surface from the film's opening moments. Bonnie's enticing nakedness in her bedroom, Clyde's bouncing phallic toothpick, Bonnie's seductive soda drinking and her salacious caress of Clyde's strategically placed pistol, her mauling of Clyde as he drives the getaway car, all charge the film with a pervasive eroticism which seems destined to culminate in sexual intercourse immediately following the hold-up. But it doesn't. Instead, Clyde, in one of his few effective rhetorical flourishes, mesmerises Bonnie with his plans for them, capturing her with a picture of wealth and fame that makes the satisfaction of mere animal appetites pall in comparison to the world they will inhabit as glamorous criminals. What Clyde offers Bonnie stretches far beyond the physical gratification he is incapable of providing her. His captivating vision of how she can escape her drab surroundings, of who she could become and of what she deserves in this life transcend his physical failure, though his impotence will create ripples of discontent and disappointment for the rest of the picture.

Penn now cuts to a greasy, nondescript diner where Clyde tells Bonnie the story of her dreary existence as a waitress. He correctly surmises how every day she returns home from the dingy restaurant she hates, stares into the mirror and desperately wonders, 'When and how am I ever gonna get away from this?' At this point, Penn incorporates one of the subtle, soundless moments of realisation that fill this movie. An older waitress, sporting garish red hair and witlessly snapping her gum, brings the couple their food. Noticing the spit curl hugging her ear, a parallel style to Bonnie's hairdo, Clyde authoritatively tells his new partner, 'I don't like that. Change it.' She obediently complies. The figure of the older waitress contains the potential future of Bonnie Parker if she refuses to alter her fate. Her life will consist of greasy food and dumb truck drivers, a joyless existence that will extinguish all the sparks of creativity and intelligence she clearly possesses. Given this fleshy prophecy, we immediately understand why Bonnie opts for crime over tedium, no matter what the consequences. They exit the restaurant, steal another car and head down the road.

'We Rob Banks': On the Road with Bonnie and Clyde

This short sequence extends some of the ideas expressed in the early scenes and establishes a visual construction that dominates the film and, in fact, has already appeared in previous scenes: windows and mirrors. While he claims that he sleeps outside to stand guard, Clyde clearly hesitates to put himself in a situation that might suggest the possibility of physical intimacy. His sexual hesitancy, however, is replaced by a swaggering bravado when he talks about his prowess with a weapon. For Clyde, this expertise and marksmanship compensates for his lack of sexual potency. One could even view the escalating violence that ensues as his most powerful means of establishing a sense of traditional manhood and his most effective strategy for keeping Bonnie by his side. The breaking of glass comes to represent the fragile boundary between the inside and the outside worlds inhabited by the Barrow gang as opposed to their enemies and fans. Earlier, we saw Bonnie's fascination

with her own visage in the bedroom mirror, and this preoccupation with style and image will grow as the film evolves. At this point, however, both images are underplayed and seem more naturalistic than expressionistic.

Finally, there is Clyde's braggadocio introduction of their occupation: 'We rob banks.' Of course, they have not yet robbed a bank, and their initial attempt in the next segment will be a conspicuously comic failure. It is more important to note that Clyde spontaneously identifies with the dispossessed homeowners forced by the banks to relinquish their property, pack up their families, cram their belongings into dilapidated trucks and set out in search of a place to make a living. Throughout the film, Clyde and his gang make clear distinctions between people and institutions. The latter represent a faceless, heartless expression of governmental ineptitude and failure, the former the human face of this political tragedy. Thus, their bank robberies represent more than simple greed or even economic desperation; they symbolise a frontal attack on the cruel policies that have humiliated the people and destroyed the backbone of rural America's social and economic organisation.

'There Ain't No Money Here': The Farmers State Bank Robbery

Penn constructs this first foray into bank robbery along decidedly comic lines, but the responses of the characters reveal much about their personalities. Clyde is jumpy and jittery, obviously nervous. Penn undercuts his natty outfit by inserting an errant collar point that sticks straight out, giving him the appearance of a freshly scrubbed little boy self-consciously awkward in his best Sunday outfit. Bonnie, on the other hand, has exchanged the flimsy, sexually suggestive beige dress with the plunging V-neck collar she wore in the first scenes for a far more sophisticated ensemble: stylish, high-neck grey sweater, jaunty midnight blue beret and matching blue scarf with grey lines and patterns. With her perfectly coiffed hair and flawless make-up, she is clearly dressing for success in her new profession. (Where she found these clothes in backwater Texas remains a mystery.)

Besides the obvious social commentary concerning the failed bank which 'guarantees' its customers fiscal security, two elements in this short sequence remain important: the characters' response to the miscalculation and Penn's continuation of the glass imagery. By dragging the teller out to Bonnie waiting in the car, Clyde demonstrates that impressing her remains his foremost objective. Whether by spinning dreams, robbing banks or shooting guns, Clyde continually strives to compensate for his lack of sexual prowess, here forcing the bank clerk to absolve him of responsibility for this mistake. Bonnie, with her greater sense of the absurd and deeper personal perspective, immediately grasps the irony of the situation, while Clyde remains fixated on more concrete concerns: their financial condition.

The most interesting visual moment in this sequence occurs as Clyde hauls out the clerk to explain the mishap to Bonnie. Penn keeps the audience inside the bank looking through the window at what is going on outside, again framing an essentially silent scene. He never allows us to hear the explanation and forces us to view the interaction played on a screen limited by the parameters of the bank window. So, in effect, he stages a silent film moment within a contemporary talking film: we watch the action through two distinct screens, one inside the theatre and one inside the frame's action. And, of course, Clyde's destruction of the bank window, with its fraudulent claims of fiscal stability and capital ($70,000), essentially breaks the transparent wall that had earlier been established between actors and audience. He literally shatters the theatrical illusion, simultaneously exploding the artistic construct (the screen within a screen) and the social deception (financial protection).

'I Ain't Against Him': The Grocery Store Robbery

This brief scene initiates the slow escalation of violence in the film. In Clyde's earlier hold-up of Ritters grocery, as well as his firing bullets into the windows of the abandoned farmhouse and the failed Farmers Bank, no one was hurt. Here, however, there is a victim, though no one is killed – yet. During the robbery, Clyde fails to understand that he is stealing from the same type of people with whom he claimed allegiance earlier, those blue-collar workers desperately trying to eke out a meagre living and avoid bank foreclosure on their property. His boyish grin as he nonchalantly waves the gun and presses the store clerk for peach pie presents his disingenuous illusion of himself as a dutiful husband out shopping for the wife and kids at the corner store. So it totally shocks

Violence in the film steadily escalates until the final explosion of bullets

him when the butcher attempts to chop off his hand and refuses to let him leave the store with the bread, dozen eggs, quart of milk and four fried pies he has forced the clerk to stuff into a paper bag. Clyde's inability to grasp how his actions contradict his ideals, to understand why a man he is robbing might be driven to attack him, provides ample evidence of his lack of self-awareness, as well as his consummate skill in deluding both himself and others about the motivations which drive his endeavours.

'Dirt In the Fuel Line': Enter C.W. Moss

Most commentators note that this scene serves simply to advance the plot: the enlistment of C.W. Moss (Michael Pollard) as surrogate son and gang member. But it also provides a rich example of Penn's unobtrusive, fluid visual style. Take, for example, how the director adeptly arranges, moves and then rearranges his characters via a beautifully choreographed synthesis of performer actions, editing selections, camera positions and movements. Initially, he situates Clyde in the foreground rolling a cigarette, Bonnie in midground fiddling with her hair, and C.W. in the background working on the car, with the dilapidated gas station looming above and behind all of them. Penn's choice to shoot this scene in deep focus (which keeps all the planes in focus simultaneously) intimately unites the three figures into a single, connected image, linking them with each other as they will be for the rest of the movie. The use of deep focus further allows Penn to orchestrate an intricate ballet of form and content that visually accentuates the emotional changes in the relationship between the three characters as the scene develops, but simultaneously keeps each figure tethered to the other two who share the frame.

By paying careful attention to the character arrangement, the viewer can more clearly understand how Penn's visual consciousness functions to deepen character development, reveal thematic strands and encourage audience identification. So, we see Clyde move to the background as Bonnie assumes the foreground and C.W. the midground, while a moment later the configuration shifts again with C.W. in the foreground, Bonnie the midground and Clyde the background. After a couple of individual and over-the-shoulder two-shots with C.W. and Bonnie, Penn re-establishes the initial triangular construction that opened the sequence: Clyde in foreground, Bonnie in midground, C.W. in background. These supple spatial juxtapositions add a seductive, dance-like quality to a scene in which Bonnie cajoles and Clyde dares C.W. to join them, providing a suggestive visual interplay which skilfully captures the intermeshed combination of flirtation and machismo, enticement and challenge, which will ultimately draw the three characters together into a surrogate family.

Before leaving this seemingly ordinary scene, one other visual element bears attention, as it forms a prominent component of Penn's overall visual strategy. I've already mentioned that the film's dominant visual leitmotif is the various combinations of glass and mirrors that sparkle and shatter from the first sequence until the last and within almost every scene in between, sometimes in overt and other times far more subtle ways. This scene shows how Penn subtly incorporates these images without interrupting or undercutting the realism of the moment, by using the side windows and mirrors of the car to frame and separate the characters throughout the action. First, in an over-the-shoulder two-shot, C.W. views Bonnie, who sits in the driver's seat, through a combination of the side window and side mirror. Then, Penn reverses the shot and positions the window/mirror combination to separate Bonnie and C.W. as they chat about the status of the stolen car. Finally, when Clyde climbs back into the driver's seat, Penn encircles his face and body by the passenger's side window in a tight three-shot as Clyde offers C.W. the opportunity to rob banks with them. Without calling direct attention to it, Penn continues to weave this complicated frame of mirrors and windows into the very fabric of the film.

'Where's the Car?': The Mineola Bank Robbery

From the moment Clyde shoots the Mineola bank employee (whose bloody murder visually alludes to a famous image from the 'Odessa Steps' sequence in Sergei Eisenstein's *Potemkin* [1925]), *Bonnie and Clyde* turns deadly serious and never totally returns to the carefree mood of the earlier robberies. The soundtrack cues us that this stick-up is clearly different. For one thing, the heist is not accompanied by the jocular bluegrass picking of Flatt and Scruggs, so the viewer is not emotionally encouraged to identify with Bonnie and Clyde's reckless daring. For another, the scene opens with the jarring sound of a squawking car horn that functions as a sound transition from the previous sequence of sexual frustration and leads directly to physical violence and death. Even C.W.'s slapstick attempts to extricate the getaway car provides precious little comic relief, since his choice to park in the cramped spot ultimately results in the killing of an innocent man.

'We're In the Money': At the Movies with the Barrow Gang

With this scene, Bonnie and Clyde's overt preoccupation with fashion, with their appearance, furnishes ample evidence of their self-conscious construction of a romantic, outlaw image, as do later scenes featuring a variety of picture taking (both of themselves and others, most notably Frank Hamer) and publicity stunts – including Bonnie's prophetic poem about their lives which receives extensive coverage in the newspapers across the country. In the movie theatre scene (*Gold Diggers of 1933* is on the screen), Penn juxtaposes an extravagant song and dance number (Ginger Rogers sings 'We're in the Money' to Busby Berkeley's lavish choreography) with the real tragedy that has just sealed the fate of these characters. Clyde, fully aware of the consequences of his actions, alternately threatens, berates, hits and chastises C.W. for his foolish decision. Bonnie, however, is far more taken with the fantasy on the screen than the reality which envelops them, preferring glamorous illusion to dismal reality.

Penn archly uses the dazzling Berkeley number to comment on the turn of events caused by Clyde's slaying of the bank teller in Mineola. Busby Berkeley was the pre-eminent creator of escapist entertainment during the darkest days of America's Depression. Such breezy entertainment allowed disheartened Americans to forget their financial troubles for a few buoyant hours at the movie theatre. *Gold Diggers of 1933* was the first of five Warner musicals based on a play by Avery Hopwood in which a feisty group of girls search for millionaire husbands. Ironically, it spotlights just the type of life Clyde promised Bonnie the day they met; at this point, however, he has only provided her with seedy motel rooms, small-time bank robberies and now a murder. But, Bonnie remains mesmerised by the image, rather than the reality, of their lives together. Transfixed by the elaborate fantasy dancing across the screen, she prefers the fiction to the facts. The inherently self-referential structure of viewers watching characters in a film as those characters simultaneously watch another film about other characters establishes a delicate interplay between the fictional crime narrative on our moviescreen as compared and contrasted to the fictional musical being watched by Bonnie, C.W. and Clyde. Penn draws our attention to

Berkeley's ornate construct within his film, wryly commenting on his own creation flickering in front of our own eyes.

'Not a Minute's Peace': The Motel Blues

Besides the plot factors evident here, this scene provides another good example of Penn's adroit manipulation of the space surrounding Bonnie and Clyde to convey their emotional and psychological state. In particular, it shows how he consistently narrows the parameters of the frame to establish an acute visual sense of his characters being caged, both physically and psychologically. Look, for example, at his framing of the segment in which Clyde offers to provide Bonnie with a way home. She sits on the bed, trapped between the door and the window. He communicates with her from the adjoining room, equally squeezed between door and wall. In both cases, Penn pinches in the borders of the frame, visually confining his characters within a cramped space, situated within a larger open space, that indicates their restricted mental and emotional condition. Even when Bonnie and Clyde function within relatively open spaces, Penn often creates a *mise en scène* that constricts their actions and provides a visual equivalent to their psychological condition.

As the film progresses, Clyde's impotence, a subject almost totally ignored in prior films, provides a new way to explore the intimate link between sex and violence. Struggling to find alternative ways to demonstrate his manhood and thus not lose Bonnie's love, Clyde ratchets up the illegal thrills until the inevitable tragedy overtakes them. From the first scene until the film's final moments, therefore, sex and violence are intrinsically tied together. In earlier script drafts the sexual dynamics were even more radical: Clyde was presented as a homosexual and a *ménage à trois* between Bonnie, Clyde and C.W. Moss (complete with a mini orgy in a motel) was included.

'Ain't Life Grand': The Arrival of Buck and Blanche

Buck (Gene Hackman) and Blanche (Estelle Parsons), Clyde's older brother and his wife, are the final members of the Barrow gang and their arrival solidifies the surrogate family structure: Bonnie and Clyde as mother and father; Buck as the jolly, backslapping uncle; Blanche as the prissy and annoying aunt; C.W. as the rather dimwitted youngster. Throughout the remainder of the film, Penn will stage an elaborate series of interconnected scenes with these five characters, rotating them in a succession of shifting alignments, carefully moving them in and out of various combinations with each other. The inclusion of Buck and Blanche also establishes a tension that will gnaw at the intimate link between Bonnie and Clyde. Often, Clyde will be forced to choose between his connection to Buck by blood and to Bonnie by love, decisions that leave him little room for compromise without alienating either his brother or his lover. Perhaps even more importantly, Bonnie and Clyde will only rarely be shown alone from this point forward in the film – the most prominent exceptions being the lovemaking scene in the field and the climactic ending. For Clyde, the arrival of Buck and Blanche seems a positive development, since it provides less opportunities for possible sexual failure. For Bonnie, however, their intrusion represents a major shift in her symbiotic relationship with Clyde and an interruption of their special bond.

Penn also continues to develop his use of staged visual images that depict highly constructed self and public images as an important part of the film's thematic structure. As scriptwriter David Newman says: 'What first attracted us … was hearing about the photos they took of each other … the business of Bonnie posing with a cigar and so on.'[42] In the previous scene, Clyde's embarrassing failure to consummate his sexual relationship with Bonnie left him with a severely bruised ego and a disappointed partner. Here, he bolsters his sagging self-image by assuming a jaunty pose on the car's front bumper cradling a machine gun. (The directions in the script describe him as 'posing like a movie tough'.) The inclusion of a bigger gun seems an obvious overcompensation for his failure to achieve an erection. Bonnie's consciously struck pose is even more suggestive of her inner conflicts. By stripping Clyde of both his cigar and his pistol, accoutrements traditionally associated with men, she forcefully assumes the masculine role. But her sensuous pose on the car hood – drawing back her jacket, thrusting her breasts forward, separating her legs and hiking up her skirt, with the gun resting on her hip, and her left arm draped over the headlight – presents an arresting image of bold sexuality unfettered by the socially acceptable demands of feminine docility. These two sides of Bonnie's personality battle for dominance throughout the rest of the picture.

'The Laws are Outside': The Joplin Shoot-out

The Joplin sequence sets up a dramatic pattern of alternating domestic scenes and fierce gun battles that dominates the central portion of the

Bonnie uses staged scenes to construct the gang's public image

film. Yet, even within the quieter scenes that show this pseudo-family at rest, personal tensions and emotional flare-ups rarely allow the characters much respite from their bloodier activities. Clyde, as already mentioned, uses the constant presence of Buck and Blanche to avoid any possible further sexual failures with Bonnie. She gets little peace from the irritating presence of others always surrounding them. To complicate matters, Bonnie and Blanche take an almost instant dislike to each other, forcing the brothers to choose different sides in the various disputes which arise. (Watch how Penn situates Bonnie in relation to Blanche, rarely allowing the two to face each other even within the same space.) Bonnie takes little pleasure in the simple games enjoyed by the others, and they find precious little amusement listening to her doggerel. In some ways, the violent segments that inevitably disrupt the gang's vain attempts at restful tranquillity seem like objective correlatives for the psychological and emotional pressures that build to bursting point during the pseudo-domestic scenes.

The Missouri motel shoot-out raises the level of violence considerably from previous incidents. Before, the gunfire had been limited to one or two policemen firing at a fleeing Bonnie and Clyde or characterised simply by Clyde shooting his gun into the air to frighten people. Here, however, an organised pack of policemen blockade the driveway in an attempt to corner the gangsters. The sheer magnitude of the firepower also increases. Entering the apartment, Clyde deposits a wooden crate loaded with an assortment of high-powered weapons they have somehow managed to collect in their travels across various states. Later, during the actual gun battle, he and the others fire a variety of these guns and rifles with deadly accuracy. The actual length of the battle is the longest shooting sequence in the movie up to this point and, as we have come to expect, punctuated by shattered windows and flying glass.

The relatively short scene in which, following their escape, Bonnie and Clyde argue is important because it stands as one of the few times these characters actually articulate their worst feelings for each other. Clyde angrily reveals that Bonnie has no right to castigate Blanche as ignorant, as she was 'just a West Dallas waitress spending half your time picking up truck drivers'. She bitterly responds by assaulting his sexuality: 'Big Clyde Barrow. … The only thing special about you is your peculiar ideas about lovemakin, which is no lovemakin at all.' Both characters suddenly realize they have gone too far, attacking each other's most cherished self-delusions. Look, for example, at Clyde's gestures as Bonnie attempts to draw them back from this emotional precipice: he puts up his arms as if protecting himself from the physical blows of an attacker. Slowly, he opens his fists, reaching down to caress her hair and face. They have pulled back from the edge.

'Take His Picture': Enter Captain Frank Hamer

Captain Frank Hamer (Denver Pyle) personifies the legal and social forces amassing to crush Bonnie and Clyde – and all they represent. Even though Clyde taunts him about neglecting his real duty ('protecting the rights of poor folks, not chasing the Barrow gang') and brags about how the public shields them ('you're supposed to be protecting them from us and they're protecting us from you'), Hamer maintains an impassive silence in the face of this insulting harangue. Bonnie's lingering kiss, however, pushes him beyond the limits of his contemptuous stoicism, and he erupts into the only moment of passion he exhibits throughout the entire film. Hamer never sees Bonnie as a beautiful and desirable woman. With her unrestrained sexuality, usurpation of male prerogatives, appealing criminality, humorous vitality and clever perversity, Bonnie embodies the impending social chaos held precariously in place by the rigid moral and legal codes that configure his personal and professional existence: Hamer's relentless pursuit of the anarchistic Barrow gang makes him the cinematic equivalent to Javert in Victor Hugo's *Les Misérables*, an equally humourless man obsessed with the letter and not the spirit of the law.

Unswayed by any notion of the conviviality or romanticism of the Barrow gang, he must exterminate them before their intoxicating liberation infects the foundations of his conventional society.

This segment also reveals the gang's growing realisation that verbal language and visual images can be manipulated to create their persona. When Buck recites the newspaper's outlandish account of their supposed escapades, stories accusing them of robberies so geographically distant from each other (from New Mexico to Illinois, from Indiana to Texas) that they would be physically impossible to accomplish, they delight in their expanding notoriety. The newspaper accounts meld them into stock figures from dime novels and Saturday matinee serial adventure: 'the will-of-the-wisp bandit Clyde Barrow' and 'his yellow-haired companion Bonnie Parker'. To the public, therefore, the members of the Barrow gang have become characters in an unfolding melodrama, shimmering figures quite similar to the chorus girls in the Busby Berkeley film glimpsed earlier. Later, Clyde comes to understand that such exaggerations strengthen the repressive forces of society out to destroy them. By purposefully embellishing the gang's criminal activities, and thereby magnifying their threat to society, the lawmen who apprehend them will enhance their own reputations and convince the public to support even more restrictive rules and confining regulations.

At this point, however, Bonnie's instinctual grasp of media manipulation effectively serves the gang's desire to discourage bounty hunters from pursing them across state boundaries. As David Newman observes: 'Their skill at creating "images" for the public could have got them the Coca-Cola account today.'[43] Early in the segment, Blanche casually snaps shots of nature and her fellow outlaws, innocent actions reminiscent of the playful picture-taking prior to the Joplin shoot-out. But Bonnie's scheme to take their photograph with the unfortunate Hamer, to humiliate him so totally that 'he's gonna wish he was dead', demonstrates a decidedly contemporary understanding of how the media and celebrities feed off each other: the Barrow gang generates headlines that increase readership; in return, the newspapers make them famous and, perhaps, even immortal. Bonnie grasps precisely how cunning image construction will convey a message they seek to communicate to lawmen throughout the country, as well as to the general public. Clearly, the gang cannot simply ask bounty hunters to leave them

Bonnie instinctively grasps how the media can be manipulated

alone, but by posing with Hamer they can dramatically illustrate the perils that await those who aspire to apprehend the Barrow gang.

Finally, the arrival of Hamer signals a fusing of genres that fashions *Bonnie and Clyde* into an intriguing cinema hybrid. Until this point, the film draws most of its essential imagery and plot line from crime/gangster movies, even though its rural settings seem far removed from the traditional city landscape that characterises that urban genre. Here, however, elements of the western become far more apparent. Clyde's dexterous blasting of Hamer's gun from his hand is staged like a western-style showdown. Hamer, as a Texas ranger, is a familiar stock character from western films. His Stetson hat, which Bonnie plops on her head, and his six-shooter, which she appropriates to stroke his moustache with the barrel, seem like familiar props dropped into the movie from an earlier era and a different genre. Eventually, Hamer even gathers together a posse to ambush Bonnie and Clyde. By incorporating essential iconographic elements from the western, the film moves beyond the footprint of a mere cops-and-robbers chase; its shift in texture and tone partakes of the mythic American struggle, chronicled in generation after generation of westerns, between outsiders and society, between rugged individualists and the forces of civilisation that strive to tame them.

'Times Is Hard': The Barrow Gang at Work
This segment furthers two meaningful elements in the film. First, the gang exhibits an expertise that befits their increasing status as fabled outlaws. Buck's athletic leap over the high grille, Clyde's precise

marksmanship when the guard draws on him, Bonnie's calm sophistication and C.W.'s wary protection outside the building all demonstrate the smooth coordination of assigned tasks necessary to execute a professional bank job. Yet Penn undercuts their adeptness at taking the money with irony in the later section of the sequence: the small amount they actually steal and the internal bickering that accompanies its distribution seem more appropriate to amateurs than to legendary criminals. Clyde's weary attempt to pacify both Bonnie and Buck (by giving his wife a share) places him in the uncomfortable role of again choosing between a family member and a lover, behaviour guaranteed to grind down his authority, while creating even greater dissension and frustration among the gang's members. His lecture to Bonnie about responsibilities towards one's family is met with hostile comments about the needs of her own family.

Given these developments, this segment provides a sobering behind-the-scenes look at outlaws on the run. Penn deftly contrasts the glamorous and exciting vision of fugitive life in the public's mind, that intoxicating bouillabaisse of unrealistic images inspired by fanciful scriptwriters and the reporters, with a far more squalid and mundane portrait of their actual existence, consisting of petty arguments, run-down motels and chilly nights in the woods. And to what end? As usual, the more astute Bonnie sees the underlying pattern blurred by the monotony of their daily events. She understands that the pointless cycle of crimes which circumscribes their lives has destroyed their freedom as effectively as any lengthy prison sentence. With disillusionment and frustration dripping in her voice, she asks Clyde: 'But, where can we go now? We rob the damn banks. What else do we do?' 'Well, what do you want to do?' he responds, not comprehending Bonnie's dissatisfaction with their way of life. For him, robbing the banks is the endpoint; for her, the thefts should lead to something more. Bonnie's question hangs unanswered in the air with no easy or apparent answer, interrupted by C.W.'s insistence that they must find a new automobile to replace their broken one.

Second, and contributing to Penn's persistent scrutiny of fame and notoriety in the film, everyone connected with this robbery, on both sides of the law, remains highly conscious that being held up by Bonnie and Clyde represents a very public event that thrusts all involved into the limelight – if only for a few fleeting moments. When he enters the bank,

The Barrow gang robs another bank

Clyde proudly proclaims, 'Good afternoon, we're the Barrow gang,' an announcement that freezes people dead in their places. Later, as reporters interview him, the bank guard uses clichéd and pretentious phrases to bathe himself in the heroic glow of action heroes from B movies: 'There I was, staring square into the face of death.' Then, he buttons up his collar and primps for the news photo. Both he and the smiling bank president proudly pose for pictures while pointing to the bullet hole Clyde drilled into their wall, a concrete souvenir of their brush with the illustrious Bonnie and Clyde. It is, as the script directions tell us, 'a legacy of celebrity'. Even the good-natured Buck gets into the act. He steals a pair of sunglasses from an ancient guard, directing him to 'Take a good look, Pop. I'm Buck Barrow. We're the Barrow boys.' All the people involved in the hold-up want to manipulate how they will appear in the narrative of the heist; they want to control the creation of their image for the present and for posterity.

'Folks Just Like Us': Eugene and Velma Meet the Barrow Gang
The basically comic segment with Eugene (Gene Wilder) and Velma (Evans Evans) provides further evidence of the contradictory impulses operating within the collective psyche of the Barrow gang: their wish to blend in with other folks and their stark realisation that such anonymity is no longer an option. Romanticised bank robbers cannot simply fade back into the daily life shared by mundane citizens; mythical heroes can never become mere mortals again. Eugene and Velma function as dramatic foils to Bonnie and Clyde. They accentuate how their criminal actions, and the

publicity they generate, have forever separated Bonnie and Clyde from mainstream society. On the most basic level, the gang, starved for companionship outside their own narrow circle, kidnaps Eugene and Velma. The frightened couple provides a temporary diversion from the divisive tensions and perpetual arguments, as well as a safe respite from the crimes and killings that now dominate their existence. Even crammed uncomfortably into the overcrowded car, one stolen from the people they now welcome as their guests, the gang delights in the momentary opportunity to socialise with someone other than themselves, to make contact with people they consider to be 'just like us'. Through nearly all of this momentary interlude they depict themselves as everyday working folks. They construct an entire scenario of normal life, treating Eugene and Velma like new neighbours invited over for a convivial evening of food and conversation.

Yet this construction, on both the conscious and the unconscious level, represents another example of their self-delusional mentality. Covering their actions with a thin veneer of almost desperate sociability, the gang simply ignores the actual situation that puts them into contact with Eugene and Velma. First of all, they forced them into the car at gunpoint, so this is far from a casual evening with friends. Second, Eugene and Velma would surely not exchange extended pleasantries, and actually share a meal, with the people who stole their car, if those thieves were not the famous and terrifying Barrow gang. Eugene might also not respond so enthusiastically to the mindless 'cow story' if it were not told by Buck Barrow, who has a shotgun lying ominously across his lap. And, most importantly, Bonnie would probably not be disturbed by Eugene's profession if she were not so keenly aware of her fatal destiny. When Eugene reveals himself as an undertaker, according to the script directions, the gang's masquerade of normality immediately ceases: 'Suddenly everyone freezes. A shudder, as if the cold hand of death had suddenly touched the occupants of the car. The atmosphere changes to cold, deadly, fearful silence in exactly one second. It is a premonition of death for the Barrows, and they react accordingly, Bonnie especially.'[44]

On a visual level, director Penn continues his recurring image pattern of glass and windows as both subtle barriers and fragmentary pathways to the physical and emotional lives of the characters. Here, after the gang pushes Eugene and Velma's car off the road, they gather around making silly faces through the windows at the frightened couple. As in the earlier scene with Hamer's face jammed against the car's rear window, Penn situates us inside the car. His camera placement forces us to share Eugene and Velma's extremely nervous point of view. (Later, during the Oakies camp sequence, a severely wounded Bonnie and Clyde lie almost unconscious in the backseat as curious onlookers gape at them through the car's windows.)

Penn constantly shifts our visual point of reference and identification, while maintaining an image construction persistently mediated by glass. From the first scene until the last, we watch people either through or starring at others trapped within windows, the glass representing a thin barrier between the inevitably hostile worlds represented by the characters and their values. Even more importantly, this visual embodiment of being on display, of always being under overt scrutiny and of never being able to hide or go unrecognised, becomes a significant visual technique used to demonstrate Bonnie and Clyde's isolation from everyday folks and their evolution into mythic figures. As this transformation occurs, the gangster couple progressively forfeits its private life. They remain under a constant state of observation, either by law enforcers eager to capture them or by common people anxious to share a moment of their fame. They endure as public figures condemned as much by their notoriety as by their crimes. Unlike Eugene and Velma, Bonnie and Clyde will never neck peacefully on a swing sitting upon an open front porch, for they can never be fully hidden from the prying eyes that seek to exploit and destroy them.

'I Wanna See My Mama': Cornfield Revelations

The encounter with Eugene and Velma convinces Bonnie that her violent death is inevitable and, perhaps, not too far in the future, so she desperately wants to visit her ageing mother before one of them dies. Within this short, visually beautiful and emotionally moving scene, Penn effectively uses the surrounding environment, particularly the natural imagery, to convey the emotional life of his characters. Several commentators, most notably John Cawelti, clarify how the seasonal cycle accompanies the developing story.[45] Such use of the seasons and their inherent connotations has been an integral element of narrative art since Greek and Roman literature, not to mention the Bible. Yet, Penn subtly blends these natural elements into his images. By never calling attention

Natural imagery often symbolises internal emotions in the film

to their inclusion, nor making them conspicuously symbolic, they seem organic to the story, rather than incorporated to make a statement.

This brief scene also contains one of my favourite visual moments in the entire movie: as Clyde desperately races across the parched cornfield after the retreating Bonnie, Penn's camera captures their despair and urgency in the film's most unobstructed and stunning long shot. It remains one of the few images not bound by the restrictive image patterns and, therefore, startles the viewer with its expansive scope. Yet even here, Penn severely undercuts this visual freedom by surrounding the couple with shadowy images of destruction. Out of nowhere an enormous black cloud sweeps across the desolate field, bathing nature and the characters in almost total darkness. In the interview I conducted with Penn, he told me that, as he shot this scene, a cloud unexpectedly shrouded the sun to give him that melancholy image of gloom soaking up the light as it moves inexorably across the rows of decaying corn stalks. He called it a 'lucky accident of filmmaking'. Planned or not, the image powerfully foreshadows the couple's ultimate demise, as if the angel of death is stalking them and blotting out any light in their lives.

'You'd Best Keep Running': The Family Reunion
Like the scene with Eugene and Velma, the family gathering demonstrates the gang's efforts to reconnect, on some fundamental level, with everyday society, this time Bonnie's relatives rather than total strangers. And, like the earlier attempt, it ends with harsh reality trumping their self-deluding fantasies of being just like everyone else.

Penn bathes the scene in the dream-like glow of slightly hazy images and muffled sounds, a romanticised montage of warm impressions and homey moments that provide the illusion of integration back into the family structure. But even Clyde's charming bravado cannot match Mrs Parker's common-sense reality. When he calls Bonnie his 'little girl' and assures her mother that he 'won't risk her to make money', the only response is strained credulity. When Clyde revs up the rhetoric to claim that, when the difficult financial times end, they will settle down and live no more than three miles away from 'her precious mother', Mrs Parker bluntly deflates his manufactured nonsense: 'You try to live three miles from me and you won't live long, honey. You'd best keep running, Clyde Barrow, and you know it.' This final reunion with her family forces Bonnie to accept that life with Clyde is now the only option available to her. In the closing moments of the scene, Bonnie sadly watches her family leave, reaches out for Clyde's protective arm, and pulls herself up against his sheltering body. This is where she belongs now.

Penn told me that, technically, this scene was unlike any other in the film. For example, he plays with time in it. He overcranks (shot at about eighteen frames per second) the child falling down the hill, after another child pretends to shoot him, so it became 'an adumbration to foreshadow the ending. It was just to say, wait a minute, time changes here just a bit.' He also positions his characters quite differently than elsewhere, using open spaces in contrast to his more usual construction of enclosed environments. Look how he pastes C.W., standing guard atop a hill, against the expansive blueness of the open sky, a moment repeated

A picnic: the gang attempts to participate in everyday life

later as Clyde brings him food and tucks a napkin under his chin. Thematically, Penn intended the scene to show 'that the real family had now faded into the position of the photograph. It had no more reality than the photograph.' But it goes further. Even for the family, Bonnie and Clyde have evolved into public figures, though Clyde warns them not to believe all they read: 'If we done half of that stuff they say in the papers, we'd be millionaires by now.' Yet the family members reverently save headlines about them in a scrapbook; they pose for home photographs, eagerly capturing their moment with the celebrities and pretending to apprehend the fugitives. Even the banter points to their conspicuous differences. When one relative asks Clyde, 'Where are you headed to?' Clyde responds, 'At this point, we ain't headed nowhere. We're just running from.' Bonnie and Clyde have no home and, as this scene reveals, no family beyond themselves. Their choices set them upon a course of events as inexorable as a Greek tragedy and with much the same results: 'That's the Laws talkin there,' Clyde tells Mama Parker. 'They want us to look big, so they'll look big when they catch us.'

'I'm Your Family Now': The Platte City Shoot-out

Unlike the Joplin shoot-out, the Platte City ambush and its continuation around Dexter takes a notable toll on the decidedly outnumbered Barrow gang. Buck and Blanche are severely wounded; one will soon die and the other be rendered blind. Both battles also spotlight the escalation of violence, a stylistic visual presentation clearly inspired by images of carnage in Vietnam seen daily in living rooms across the United States.

A dying Buck Barrow surrounded by the law

The carnage in Vietnam,
seen nightly on television
sets, informed Penn's
screen violence

Perhaps the most significant visual difference is that the Joplin shoot-out takes place during the day, while Platte City's bloodshed occurs at night, as Penn immerses the viewer in the sheer panic and almost total confusion experienced by the gang members. We are never certain who is firing at whom and what is happening throughout the sequence. Penn accentuates the havoc of the encounter when he straps his inside camera on the ceiling of the fleeing car, capturing the panic and cramped chaos of the trapped and wounded gangsters.

In the field outside of Dexter, the Barrow gang is forever destroyed. The forces of society unleashed by their antisocial acts will stop at nothing to crush them and the freedom they have come to represent. Penn's visual construction depicts the gang as defenceless victims of the powerful cultural and ideological forces aligned to subdue them, helplessly circling inside a deadly shooting gallery. The lawmen's savage demolition of the second car, accompanied by Indian war whoops and spontaneous yelps of pleasure, lets us experience their abandonment to the irrational and uncontrolled overuse of violence (which will culminate in the final ambush). The scene's tone harkens back to countless westerns where the horse, shot out from under its rider, renders the man vulnerable on the ground and without a means of either escape or attack. Penn has now conducted us along an accelerating path of intensifying violence from Clyde practising his marksmanship with a swinging tyre to this intense fire fight complete with weapons of war. As Bonnie, Clyde and C.W. hobble away at the scene's conclusion, the now hesitant strains of 'Foggy Mountain Breakdown' become a sad reminder of the jocular early days, the far simpler times, and the immeasurably more innocent events that preceded this horrifying ferocity.

'Are They Famous?': The Oakie Camp Site

Penn's visual construction of the Oakie camp site quickly establishes the numbing poverty, acute need and innate dignity of these refugees, displaced victims of America's economic collapse. He sets up the brief sequence with an elegantly composed long shot emphasising the temporary quality of the camp, as well as its juxtaposition to the more permanent forms of nature, in this case a lake stretching out beyond the limits of the frame. The battered cars and trucks, bulging with whatever goods can be squeezed into and tied down on top of them, sit loosely arranged in a ragged circle around several campfires. Clothing hung out to dry flaps incessantly in the arid wind. The blank faces of the children and their parents betray their emotional disorientation, their stunned awareness that the country's economic misfortune has driven them off the land and into a desperate search for work. Forced to abandon their homes for promises of employment, however faint, they must migrate to faraway places that will ultimately offer little more than a temporary refuge from the overwhelming poverty and despair that has overtaken them.

Even here, among people burdened by their own dire problems, even in their feeble and totally vulnerable condition, the criminals still remain celebrities capable of drawing a crowd of gaping onlookers. As C.W. gently holds up the cup of water to Bonnie's lips, Penn places the camera outside the car, forcing us to peer into the backseat through the front windshield, once again drawing in the edges of the frame. A teenage girl directly opposite our point of view peeks at the couple through the back window, so they remain pinioned between her gaze and that of the audience. As the other Oakies quietly gather around the car, we witness their hesitant gawking, the camera maintaining a steady field of vision encompassing both the frail couple and their curious observers. One man hesitantly pokes his hand through the side window and nudges Clyde's finger, delicately checking to see if he is still alive and how it feels to touch a famous man. Clyde barely responds, other than weakly opening his eyes. Bonnie and Clyde will never again attain the power, freedom and energy they had earlier in the movie. Their slumped and bloodied figures attest to the strength of the socially sanctioned forces allied against them, a powerful collaboration of morality and violence that will inevitably destroy them.

'What's That On Your Chest?': Malcolm Moss's Farm
The most significant aspect of this short scene is Malcolm Moss's forceful reaction to his son's tattoo, which affronts his moral sensibilities and transgresses beyond the bounds of acceptable behavior. Screenwriter David Newman contextualises his response by comparing it to the generation clash which characterised the 60s:

> Just as our parents were 'offended' by long hair, Woodstock, rock and roll, smoking pot and dropping out, we reflected this by inventing the tattoo on C.W.'s chest that directly leads to the assassination of Bonnie and Clyde. ... And it is because of that (*and only that*) that Malcolm rats out the luckless couple and sets up their ambush. Because his sense of propriety was offended by their flaunting of a freakish style. Sounds like the Sixties?[46]

The screenwriters' invention of C.W.'s tattoo, and its ultimately fatal consequences for Bonnie and Clyde, directly link the Barrow gang's defiance of conventional societal standards in the 30s and the youthful rebellion which challenged cultural mores and established institutions in the 60s.

'I Come Here to Question Blanche Barrow': The Texas Ranger and the Preacher's Daughter
While the segments between the jail cell/hospital room that holds Blanche and Malcolm's farm function mainly to advance the plot, Penn's

C.W.'s father angrily
responds to his tattoo

choice to break up the Hamer/Blanche interrogation with the farmhouse section calls attention to the interconnections between the two settings and the characters who inhabit them. So, while this narrative tactic accentuates the simultaneity of the actions, it concurrently stresses the vast differences between Hamer's relentless pursuit and the couple's vulnerable position at Malcolm's farmhouse. Hamer deceives Blanche, making her trust him by offering empathetic commiseration for her plight and laying total blame for Buck's death on Bonnie and Clyde, a scenario the distraught Blanche willingly accepts. She hungers to be heard and understood. Similarly, Malcolm lulls Bonnie and Clyde into a false, and finally fatal, sense of security by feigning a similar sympathy with their situation. They, too, yearn to be heard and understood. Once away from their sight, however, he continues his fierce barrage of invectives about C.W.'s tattoo, referring to it, as well as to Bonnie, as 'cheap trash'. Not surprisingly, these two emotional manipulators and shrewd liars will ultimately conspire to lure Bonnie and Clyde to their death.

The scene also contains our last image of Blanche Barrow, a partially comic, partially tragic, partially pathetic figure disastrously entangled in dramatic and violent events far beyond her narrow range of control. She sits, swaddled in a white hospital gown and hugging a snowy blanket on her lap, caged in an antiseptic hospital room with metal webbing on the windows and door. She is encased by bandages from the top of her head to beneath her lacerated eyes. The brightly lit room, as stark and pallid as Blanche's sanitary dressing, contains only the barest

Blanche Barrow questioned by the relentless Captain Frank Hamer

fragments of domestic refuge: a bed, chest of drawers, night table and chairs – all monotonous, standard-issue hospital furniture. In essence, this austere space represents a more spartan version of all those seedy motel lodgings Blanche shared uncomfortably with the gang, though its uncluttered sterility renders this room far more bleak than the cosy shabbiness of Platte or Joplin. Her physical surroundings matter only to us, however, for Blanche Barrow can no longer see them.

One can look at this forlorn image of blindness on several levels. Limitations of sight, the partial or total lack of vision, remains another of Penn's leitmotifs throughout the film: from the opening scene with Bonnie glancing at herself in the bedroom mirror, to Clyde glimpsing Bonnie obscured by the upstairs window, to the shooting of the Mineola bank manager in the eye, to bullets shattering windows and smashing mirrors, to car headlights (resembling eyeballs) being destroyed, to lawmen shooting Buck in the face and rendering him unable to see, and finally to Clyde wearing broken sunglasses in the last scene. As another component of this ongoing visual pattern, Blanche's blindness appears both dramatically and imagistically appropriate. On a more metaphoric level, however, Blanche's sight has been extinguished by the reflected radiance of Bonnie and Clyde's exaggerated personae. She has been irrevocably scarred by her brush with fame, forever maimed by her intimate bond with two luminous figures levitated into mythological status by a voracious press and a gullible populace hungry for heroes – and for sacrificial scapegoats. Penn's last, poignant image of her, the door slowly shutting her off from the world as she prattles on about her misfortunes to an empty room, is a sadly symbolic summation of Blanche's entire existence.

'You Told My Story': Sex, Poems and Betrayal

As in the previous scene, where he interrupted Hamer's interrogation of Blanche by cutting back to the Moss household, Penn fractures Bonnie and Clyde's lovemaking by transporting us to the main street of Arcadia. And, as in that last instance, this rupture in the linear flow compels us to scrutinise characters and incidents in each setting as intricately entwined elements which continually contextualise and comment upon each other. Here, for example, Penn's narrative manoeuvre severely undercuts our ability to share the couple's exhilarating consummation of their physical relationship, compelling us to realise (at least retrospectively) that this ecstatic moment simultaneously contains the origin of their destruction. By inserting the deadly alliance between conservative society (Malcolm) and legalised violence (Hamer) in the middle of their single moment of physical fulfilment, Penn forces viewers to distance themselves from Bonnie and Clyde and refuses us even a brief moment of shared affection, unalloyed pleasure and emotional identification with these characters.

Bonnie's poem represents her last attempt to convey the couple's narrative from their own viewpoint, rather than ceding the power of the storyteller to newspaper reporters or lawmen. As such, she compares the couple to Jesse James, says that Clyde was 'honest and upright and clean', complains about the cops who disrupt their domestic life, and even foretells their eventual deaths. By cementing their tale into words, presenting their slant on the events that occurred and making their perspective the dominant interpretative paradigm, Bonnie actively configures the couple's public persona, much as she previously constructed their image via staged pictures and stylised clothing. But she also does something more. As Clyde so readily recognises, the published poem makes him 'somebody they gonna remember'. This intimation of immortality acts like a powerful dose of Viagra for the previously impotent Clyde, arousing him sufficiently to make love to Bonnie, accompanied by the equally revived tempo of 'Foggy Mountain Breakdown'.

Everyone associated with *Bonnie and Clyde* agrees that François Truffaut, the French New Wave director originally offered the script, conceived the structure of the poem-reading sequence in which Bonnie's recitation of the verse splices together the passage of time across several disparate images: beginning with the car resting in the rain, continuing with Hamer reading the verse, moving to a newspaper page containing the printed poem and concluding with the couple picnicking in a deserted field on a sunny day. Matthew Bernstein's essay on the evolution of the script demonstrates how Truffaut suggested a 'Hitchcockian way' of cutting to various shots as Bonnie speaks the words and how this technique visualises 'the mythologizing power of Bonnie's poetry'.[47] As Newman and Benton relate in their essay, 'Lightning in a Bottle', Truffaut furnished the screenwriters with an 'invaluable education in the art of the cinema', demonstrating to them 'the difference between "real time" and "film time"'. In particular, he broke down their initial

treatment into 'blocks of film which stood as emotional and dramatic entities'. By way of illustrating this principle, he also gave them the specific device of 'tying time together in film terms during Bonnie's reading of "The Ballad of Bonnie and Clyde"'.[48]

While the visual passage of time in the poem-reading sequence was Truffaut's idea, the stunning segment in downtown Arcadia, which ruptures Bonnie and Clyde's lovemaking, was unmistakably Arthur Penn. Again, the soundtrack ties together discordant images: 'Foggy Mountain Breakdown' starts as Clyde gently lowers Bonnie onto the blanket, follows the newspaper as it sails across the empty field, continues throughout the town images and conveys us back to the now satiated Bonnie and Clyde. Only then does Penn replace the bluegrass tune with lush romantic 'movie' music. In Arcadia, Penn's camera glides past a barber shop, a picture of President Roosevelt, a rusting 'Call for Phillip Morris' sign, and finally stops outside the plate-glass window of Eva's Ice Cream Parlor. (One wonders if the name consciously alludes to the biblical story of betrayal and the destruction of innocence?) Penn's graceful optical tracking shot renders the scene through a slightly hazy close-up, then refocuses to capture clearly the meeting between Malcolm and Hamer. Another subtle gesture illustrates Penn's attention to small dramatic details: when Hamer exits the ice cream store, he wipes his moustache in a manner strongly reminiscent of how Bonnie stroked it with his pistol in the picture-taking scene, a delicate visual reminder of how pervasively that event dominates his life.

'I'd Do It All Different': The Failure of Imagination
While furthering the plot, this two-shot scene in Malcolm's house once again explicitly displays the intellectual and imaginative gulf that

separates Bonnie from Clyde. Bonnie's evolution from her early days as a frustrated waitress with limited horizons to a woman with broad imaginative capabilities seems evident in her wistful conjecture about a different reality, even if such dreams remain predicated upon 'some miracle'. Now, she reflects on potentialities beyond the restrictions of their current situation, imagining what might be conceivable if they could escape from their personaes. Clyde, conversely, remains trapped within his narrow world view. Responding to Bonnie's expansive speculation, he replies only in the most mundane, concrete terms: 'I guess I'd do it all different. First off, we wouldn't live in the same state where we pull our jobs. We'd live in another state, and stay clean there. And then when we wanted to take a bank, we'd go into the other state.' For Clyde, doing it 'all different' means simply remixing the same essential ingredients in an identical stew pot. For Bonnie, it means the much grander possibility of concocting a whole range of meals other than stew.

'Time to Go Home Now': The Death of Bonnie and Clyde

Penn fills the quick scene in downtown Arcadia preceding the ambush with subtle ironies and small dramatic touches which extend the image and plot patterns he has woven throughout the film. So, for example, Bonnie and Clyde park in front of Eva's Parlor; Clyde even asks Bonnie if she wants some ice cream. They, of course, remain totally unaware that Malcolm and Hamer plotted their fate in that very same spot, but we are acutely cognisant of what transpired inside that parlour. Clyde wears sunglasses that resemble those Buck gave Blanche for her birthday, but his left lens pops out. Though he remarks jocularly that he can 'drive with one eye', the image of Clyde with one eye dark and covered, the other one clear and visible, sparks a visual recollection of the man he shot in the eye after robbing the bank in Mineola. Bonnie's fascination with the fragile porcelain shepherdess distances her from the gun-toting, fashionable, cigar-smoking criminal who shared Clyde's bank robberies. It speaks to her growing domestication and desire for a new identity, one in accord with more traditional female roles. Visually, Penn continues to pinch in the corners of the frame: C.W. peers out from the hardware store window through a narrow gap in the lace curtains; the camera captures Bonnie and Clyde from the car's backseat, restricting their (and our) vision by the contours of the front window.

Even thirty years later, the death of Bonnie and Clyde remains one of the most powerful moments in American cinema history. Penn had already experimented with changing film speeds within scenes as early as his 1957 western, *The Left-Handed Gun*: 'There we overcranked and it starts in slow motion and flips as he hits the ground; it is about eighteen frames. That cut threw me when I saw it, that one piece of weirdly timed film. It just left an impression.' By the time he came to *Bonnie and Clyde*, Penn had seen *The Seven Samurai* (1954) and readily admits that his visualisation of this scene was highly influenced by the great Japanese director, Akira Kurosawa: 'What he did was go into slow motion whenever he did a killing. I thought there was something more interesting to be done, which was change the speeds and then, through cutting, get a kind of balletic result.'

As one might imagine given the prominence of this scene in movie history, Penn has answered numerous questions about its construction and significance over the past thirty years. Basically, he conceptualised two different visualisations of death – Clyde's was to be like a ballet and Bonnie's was to have the physical shock: 'There's a moment in death when the body no longer functions, when it becomes an object and has a certain kind of detached ugly beauty. It was that aspect I was trying to get.'[49] To accomplish this, Penn set up four different cameras, each functioning at a different speed: twenty-four, forty-eight, seventy-two and ninety-six frames per second. Then, when he and editor Dede Allen shaped the final print together, they intercut between the latter three speeds (shot at faster than the normal twenty-four frames per second) to

Penn filmed Clyde's death as ballet

Bonnie's death was shot to convey physical shock

interject varying degrees of slow motion into the ambush sequence. Penn also squeezed a sizeable number of shots into a very brief time on screen, creating a frenetic montage: Prince notes that from the point when the birds fly off until the last image, a total of fifty-four seconds, Penn splices together fifty-one shots.[50] Viewers, therefore, are bombarded by almost one shot per second, a breathless pace that hypnotises us and, when it finally ceases, leaves us totally exhausted.

Earlier in this volume, I discussed the vast and influential cultural implications of the violence within *Bonnie and Clyde*, particularly epitomised by this scene. I also mentioned its connection to events during the 60s. Penn himself remarks how 'a piece of Warren's head comes off, like that famous photograph of Kennedy'.[51] Penn, as Pauline Kael so aptly put it, did 'put the sting back into death'. From a narrative perspective, the last images of Bonnie and Clyde remind us of their humanity, rather than their public personae. Bonnie, her head almost touching the ground and her arm dangling on the car's running board, bears little resemblance to a desperate criminal. Clyde, his body rolling in slow motion and his arm twisting behind his back like his brother Buck's, reminds us more of a younger brother than a brutal outlaw. The legends give way to the flesh.

Visually, Penn concludes the film with a final use of the glass-framing imagery pattern so prevalent throughout the movie. The last shot begins with the driver's side window framing the black sharecroppers and Malcolm as they edge toward the car. Penn then pans around the rear of the bullet-riddled vehicle. Finally, he stops to view the scene through the back window, cracked in its centre by a bullet hole, which is bisected by the frame of the open driver's door and its window. Only mediated in this way do we see Hamer, emotionless and dressed in black, and the other members of the posse holding their guns staring silently down at the dead bodies of their famous prey. These images, divided from each other by the various frames of glass through which we observe them, seem slightly distorted. A sparse sigh escapes from Hamer, and the frame goes to black. Only the tinkling sounds of a plaintive banjo and a mandolin lead us to the credits.

The saga of Bonnie and Clyde is over.

NOTES

1 David Newman and Robert Benton, 'Lightning in a Bottle ', in Sandra Wake and Nicola Hayden (eds), *Classic Film Scripts: Bonnie and Clyde* (New York: Frederick Ungar, 1972), p. 16.

2 Gerald Mast and Bruce F. Kawin, *A Short History of the Movies* (New York: Macmillan, 1982), p. 435.

3 Ibid., p. 441.

4 Newman and Benton, 'Lightning in a Bottle, pp. 13–14.

5 Matthew Bernstein, 'Scripting a Legend: The Writing of *Bonnie and Clyde*', forthcoming in *Film Quarterly*.

6 Ibid.

7 Ibid.

8 Peter Biskind, *Easy Riders, Raging Bulls: How the Sex-Drugs-and-Rock'n'roll Generation Saved Hollywood* (New York: Simon and Schuster, 1998), p. 24.

9 Ibid., p. 41.

10 Ibid., p. 46.

11 Ibid.

12 Ibid., p. 46.

13 For more information on the now almost forgotten Coe, see Jon Krampner, *The Man in the Shadows: Fred Coe and the Golden Age of Television* (New Brunswick: Rutgers University Press, 1998).

14 All of Arthur Penn's uncited comments in this book come from interviews I conducted with him during 1985.

15 Arthur Penn, 'Making Waves: The Directing of *Bonnie and Clyde*', in Lester D. Friedman (ed.), *Arthur Penn's Bonnie and Clyde* (New York: Cambridge University Press, 1999), p.11.

16 Ibid., p. 12.

17 David Newman, 'What's It All About?: Pictures at an Execution', in Friedman (ed.), *Arthur Penn's Bonnie and Clyde*, p. 37.

18 Penn, 'Making Waves', p. 24.

19 In his interview with me, Penn noted that his wife, Peggy Maurer Penn, a senior staff member at Ackerman Institute for Family Therapy, convinced him to switch these scenes, reasoning that Eugene's occupation as an undertaker forced death into Bonnie's consciousness and, thus, she needs to see her family because of this revelation.

20 James Davison Hunter, *Culture Wars: The Struggle to Define America* (New York: Basic Books, 1991), p. 42.

21 Page Cook, 'Bonnie and Clyde', *Films in Review*, vol. 18 no. 8, October 1967, pp. 504–5.

22 Charles Thomas Samuels, 'Bonnie and Clyde', *Hudson Review*, vol. 21 no. 1, Spring 1968, p. 22.

23 Bosley Crowther, 'Shoot-Em-Up Film Opens World Fet [*sic*]', *New York Times*, August 6, 1967, p. 32.

24 Bosley Crowther, 'Bonnie and Clyde', *New York Times*, August 14, 1967, p. 36.

25 Biskind, *Easy Riders*, p. 40.

26 Andrew Sarris, 'Bonnie and Clyde', *Village Voice*, August 24, 1967, p. 21.

27 Pauline Kael, 'Bonnie and Clyde', *The New Yorker*, October 21, 1967, pp. 147–71.

28 Biskind, *Easy Riders*, pp. 40–1.

29 Frank Beaver, *Bosley Crowther: Social Critic of Film, 1940–1967* (New York: Arno Press, 1974), p. 187.

30 For a further discussion of this controversy, see Steven Alan Carr, 'From "Fucking Cops" to "Fucking Media": *Bonnie and Clyde* for a Sixties America', in Friedman (ed.), *Arthur Penn's Bonnie and Clyde*, pp. 77–100.

31 David Cook, *A History of Narrative Film*, third edn. (New York: W.W. Norton, 1996), p. 926.

32 Penn, 'Making Waves', p. 29.

33 Glenn Man, *Radical Visions: American Film Renaissance, 1967–1976* (Westport, CN: Greenwood Press, 1994), p. 31.

34 Biskind, *Easy Riders*, p. 48.

35 Norman Mailer, *Armies of the Night* (New York: New American Library, 1968), p. 320.

36 Cook, *A History*, p. 282.

37 Stephen Prince, 'The Hemorrhaging of American Cinema: *Bonnie and Clyde*'s Legacy of Film Violence', in Friedman (ed.), *Arthur Penn's Bonnie and Clyde*, pp. 127–128.

38 Cook, *A History*, p. 919.

39 Richard Schickel, *Second Sight: Notes on Some Movies, 1965–1970* (New York: Simon and Schuster, 1972), p. 143.

40 Susan Sontag, 'The Decay of Cinema', *The New York Times Magazine*, February 25, 1996,

p. 61.

41 I am deeply indebted to Karen Bakke, chairperson of the Fashion and Retailing Department at Syracuse University for her insights into how fashion functions in *Bonnie and Clyde*.

42 Newman, 'What's It All About?', pp. 38–39

43 Ibid., p. 39.

44 Wake and Hayden (eds), *Bonnie and Clyde*, pp. 114–5.

45 John Cawelti, 'The Artistic Power of *Bonnie and Clyde*', in Cawelti (ed.), *Focus on Bonnie and Clyde* (Englewood, NJ: Prentice Hall, 1973).

46 Newman, 'What's It All About?', p. 39.

47 Bernstein, 'Scripting a Legend'.

48 Newman and Benton, 'Lightning in a Bottle', p. 20.

49 Wake and Hayden (eds), *Bonnie and Clyde*, p. 169.

50 Prince, 'The Hemorrhaging', p. 135.

51 Wake and Hayden, *Bonnie and Clyde*, p. 169.

CREDITS

· ·

Bonnie and Clyde

USA
1967

©Warner Bros.-Seven Arts
Inc/Tatira Hiller
Productions
Production Companies
Warner Bros.-Seven Arts
present
a Tatira Hiller production
Producer
Warren Beatty
Production Manager
Russ Saunders
**Assistant to the
Producer**
Elaine Michea
Director
Arthur Penn
Assistant Director
Jack N. Reddish
Script Supervisor
John Dutton
Screenplay
David Newman, Robert
Benton
Special Consultant
Robert Towne
Director of Photography
Burnett Guffey
2nd Unit Photography
Ted Saizis, Vincent Saizis
Special Effects
Danny Lee

Editor
Dede Allen
Art Director
Dean Tavoularis
Set Decorator
Raymond Paul
Costume Designer
Theadora Van Runkle
Women's Wardrobe
Norma Brown
Men's Wardrobe
Andy Matyasi
Make-up Created by
Robert Jiras
**Miss Dunaway's Make-
up**
Warner Bros. Cosmetics
Hairstylist
Gladys Witten
Music
Charles Strouse
Soundtrack
'Foggy Mountain
Breakdown' by Earl
Scruggs, perfomed by Lester
Flatt, Earl Scruggs
Sound
Francis E. Stahl
Film Extract
Gold Diggers of 1933 (1933)

Warren Beatty
Clyde Barrow
Faye Dunaway
Bonnie Parker
Michael J. Pollard
C.W. Moss
Gene Hackman
Buck Barrow
Estelle Parsons
Blanche Barrow
Denver Pyle
Captain Frank Hamer
Dub Taylor
Ivan Moss
Evans Evans
Velma Davis
Gene Wilder
Eugene Grizzard

[uncredited]
James Stiver
grocery store owner
Clyde Howdy
deputy
Garry Goodgion
Billy
Ken Mayer
Sheriff Smoot
Patrick Cranshaw

Colour by
Technicolor
10,015 feet
111 minutes

Credits compiled by
Markku Salmi,
BFI Filmographic Unit

The print of *Bonnie and
Clyde* in the National Film
and Television Archive was
acquired specially for the 360
Classics Feature Films
project from Warner Bros.
Distributors Ltd.

ALSO PUBLISHED

An Actor's Revenge
Ian Breakwell

L'Âge d'or
Paul Hammond

Annie Hall
Peter Cowie

L'Atalante
Marina Warner

L'avventura
Geoffrey Nowell-Smith

The Big Heat
Colin McArthur

The Big Sleep
David Thomson

The Birds
Camille Paglia

Blackmail
Tom Ryall

Boudu Saved from Drowning
Richard Boston

Bride of Frankenstein
Alberto Manguel

Brief Encounter
Richard Dyer

Das Cabinet des Dr. Caligari
David Robinson

Cat People
Kim Newman

Chinatown
Michael Eaton

Citizen Kane
Laura Mulvey

Double Indemnity
Richard Schickel

Les Enfants du paradis
Jill Forbes

42nd Street
J. Hoberman

"Fires Were Started –"
Brian Winston

The Ghost and Mrs Muir
Frieda Grafe

Greed
Jonathan Rosenbaum

Gun Crazy
Jim Kitses

High Noon
Phillip Drummond

In a Lonely Place
Dana Polan

It's a Gift
Simon Louvish

The Life and Death of Colonel Blimp
A.L. Kennedy

Lolita
Richard Corliss

M
Anton Kaes

The Magnificent Ambersons
V. F. Perkins

Meet Me in St. Louis
Gerald Kaufman

Napoléon
Nelly Kaplan

La Nuit américaine
Roger Crittenden

Odd Man Out
Dai Vaughan

Olympia
Taylor Downing

Palm Beach Story
John Pym

Pépé le Moko
Ginette Vincendeau

Performance
Colin MacCabe

Queen Christina
Marcia Landy and Amy Villarejo

Rocco and his Brothers
Sam Rohdie

Sanshô Dayû
Dudley Andrew & Carole Cavanaugh

The Seventh Seal
Melvyn Bragg

Shane
Edward Countryman & Evonne von Heussen-Countryman

Singin' in the Rain
Peter Wollen

Stagecoach
Edward Buscombe

Sunrise – A Song of Two Humans
Lucy Fischer

Taxi Driver
Amy Taubin

Things to Come
Christopher Frayling

Went the Day Well?
Penelope Houston

Wild Strawberries
Philip & Kersti French

The Wizard of Oz
Salman Rushdie

If you would like further information about future BFI Film Classics or about other books on film, media and popular culture from BFI Publishing, please write to:

BFI Film Classics
BFI Publishing
21 Stephen Street
London W1P 2LN

BFI Film Classics '...could scarcely be improved upon ... informative, intelligent, jargon-free companions.'
The Observer

Each book in the BFI Publishing Film Classics series honours a great film from the history of world cinema. With new titles published each year, the series is rapidly building into a collection representing some of the best writing on film. If you would like to receive further information about future Film Classics or about other books on film, media and popular culture from BFI Publishing, please fill in your name and address and return this card to the BFI.* (No stamp required if posted in the UK, Channel Islands, or Isle of Man.)

NAME

ADDRESS

POSTCODE

WHICH *BFI FILM CLASSIC* DID YOU BUY?

---

* In North America, please return your card to: Indiana University Press, Attn: LPB, 601 N. Morton Street, Bloomington, IN 47401-3797

BFI Publishing
21 Stephen Street
FREEPOST 7
LONDON
W1E 4AN